Is parenthood a right or a
privilege?

At Issue

Is Parenthood a Right or a Privilege?

Other Books in the At Issue Series:

At Issue

Is Parenthood a Right or a Privilege?

Stefan Kiesbye, Book Editor

GREENHAVEN PRESS
A part of Gale, Cengage Learning

GALE
CENGAGE Learning™

Detroit • New York • San Francisco • New Haven, Conn • Waterville, Maine • London

GALE
CENGAGE Learning

Christine Nasso, *Publisher*
Elizabeth Des Chenes, *Managing Editor*

© 2009 Greenhaven Press, a part of Gale, Cengage Learning.

Gale and Greenhaven Press are registered trademarks used herein under license.

For more information, contact:
Greenhaven Press
27500 Drake Rd.
Farmington Hills, MI 48331-3535
Or you can visit our Internet site at gale.cengage.com

For product information and technology assistance, contact us at

Gale Customer Support, 1-800-877-4253
For permission to use material from this text or product, submit all requests online at
www.cengage.com/permissions

Further permissions questions can be emailed to permissionrequest@cengage.com

Articles in Greenhaven Press anthologies are often edited for length to meet page requirements. In addition, original titles of these works are changed to clearly present the main thesis and to explicitly indicate the author's opinion. Every effort is made to ensure that Greenhaven Press accurately reflects the original intent of the authors. Every effort has been made to trace the owners of copyrighted material.

Cover image ©Images.com/Corbis.

LIBRARY OF CONGRESS CATALOGING-IN-PUBLICATION DATA

Is parenthood a right or a privilege? / Stefan Kiesbye, book editor.
   p. cm. -- (At issue)
Includes bibliographical references and index.
ISBN-13: 978-0-7377-4430-9 (hardcover)
ISBN-13: 978-0-7377-4431-6 (pbk.)
1. Parenthood--Moral and ethical aspects--Juvenile literature. I. Kiesbye, Stefan.
HQ755.8.I83 2009
306.874--dc22

                                          2009010708

Printed in the United States of America
1 2 3 4 5 6 7 13 12 11 10 09

Contents

Introduction

In Plant City, Florida, police following a lead drove to a run-down house and went inside. A woman was known to live at the address with two adult sons, but eyewitnesses had seen a small girl peering out of one window, only to disappear again.

The officers were not prepared for what they found. Lane DeGregory, from the *St. Petersburg Times*, writes, "Plant City Detective Mark Holste had been on the force for 18 years when he and his young partner were sent to the house on Old Sydney Road to stand by during a child abuse investigation. Someone had finally called the police. They found a car parked outside. The driver's door was open and a woman was slumped over in her seat, sobbing. She was an investigator for the Florida Department of Children and Families. "Unbelievable," she told Holste. "The worst I've ever seen." The police officers walked through the front door, into a cramped living room. "I've been in rooms with bodies rotting there for a week and it never stunk that bad," Holste said later. "There's just no way to describe it. Urine and feces—dog, cat and human excrement—smeared on the walls, mashed into the carpet. Everything dank and rotting." ... The floor, walls, even the ceiling seemed to sway beneath legions of scuttling roaches. "It sounded like you were walking on eggshells. You couldn't take a step without crunching German cockroaches," the detective said. "They were in the lights, in the furniture. Even inside the freezer. The freezer!"

Holste was approached by the tenant, who lived in that chaos with her two sons. Asked if she had a daughter, she answered, yes. Seven-year-old Danielle "lay on a torn, moldy mattress on the floor. She was curled on her side, long legs tucked into her emaciated chest. Her ribs and collarbone jutted out; one skinny arm was slung over her face; her black hair was matted, crawling with lice. Insect bites, rashes and sores pocked her skin. Though she looked old enough to be in school, she was naked—except for a swollen diaper."

According to the detective, who asked the mother how she could let this happen, the mother answered, "I'm doing the best I can."

Cases of child neglect and abuse abound in the national press. From babies shaken to death to seven-year-old Danielle, who will forever be disabled because of years of neglect, there seems little that parents are not able to inflict on their children. These cases are often shrugged off as acts by deranged monsters, people who somehow don't pass the test of humanity. Dr. Rahman Zamani of the California Childcare Health Program writes, "It is difficult to imagine that any person would intentionally harm a child. Many times physical abuse is a result of inappropriate or excessive physical discipline and lack of awareness of the magnitude of force applied."

The National Child Abuse and Neglect Data System estimates that in 2006 905,000 children were victims of maltreatment in the United States. Specifically, "64.1 percent of victims experienced neglect, 16.0 percent were physically abused, 8.8 percent were sexually abused, 6.6 percent were psychologically maltreated, and 2.2 percent were medically neglected. In addition, 15.1 percent of victims experienced such "other" types of maltreatment as "abandonment," "threats of harm to the child," or "congenital drug addiction." Zamani states that "Lack of parenting knowledge, unrealistic expectations of children, frequent family crises, poverty, physical disabilities, stress, lack of community support systems, substance abuse, mental health problems and domestic and other violence in the household are risk factors contributing to child abuse and neglect." And "[p]eople who were victims of abuse themselves are also more likely to be abusive too. For them it is simply the way they were raised and the only childrearing practice they are familiar with."

Can society assume that parents, without the requirement to educate themselves about child-rearing or to obtain a license, are really equipped to take care of children? Or should state or federal governments impose tests on parents-to-be, in order to ensure children's safety?

The history of the right to bear children is a colorful and varied one. From the Spartans' disposal of weak babies to the horrendous treatment of slaves; from tax credits for large families to the Chinese one-child policy—societies throughout the world have actively shaped families. And while many people find it inappropriate for states to interfere with parents' rights, American society already depends on the police and social services to take care of cases like Danielle's.

Yet the bonds within a family are often not subject to rational argument. *St. Petersburg Times* reporter Lane DeGregory reports that "Danielle's birth mother did not want to give her up even though she had been charged with child abuse and faced 20 years in prison." She finally relented, agreeing to a deal that kept her out of prison. When later interviewed, she said about the day Danielle was rescued from her house, "Part of me died that day." DeGregory writes

> She says she took Danielle to the library and the park. "I took her out for pizza. Once." But she can't remember which library, which park or where they went for pizza. . . . Michelle's older son, Bernard, told a judge that he once asked his mom why she never took Danielle to the doctor. Something's wrong with her, he remembered telling her. He said she answered, "If they see her, they might take her away."

Only adoptive parents are screened before they obtain custody of a child. If, as Zamani writes, "abused children are also more likely to become abusers and be involved in violent criminal activities later in life," then maybe society needs an open debate on family and the rights and privileges of parenthood.

1

Couples Should Need a License to Obtain the Privilege of Parenthood

Peg Tittle

Peg Tittle is a columnist for The Philosophers' Magazine *online philosophy café and the editor of* Should Parents be Licensed? Debating the Issues.

While almost every profession demands licensing, the much more challenging job of raising children requires no supervision, license, or test. Foster and adoptive parents have to undergo vigorous screening, but biological parents do not. Just because humans have the capability to have children doesn't mean they have the inherent right to procreate without supervision. Parenting, after all, is more—and more difficult—than giving birth. Life should not be created by accident, and parents should have to undergo training, then receive a parenting license—a procedure that needn't be more difficult than licensing drivers. This would save many children from being neglected, abused, and abandoned.

We have successfully cloned a sheep. It is not unreasonable, then, to believe that we may soon be able to create human life. And I'm sure we'll develop carefully considered policies and procedures to regulate the activity, perhaps if only because we have Mary Shelley's *Frankenstein* lurking in our minds.

For example, I doubt we'll allow someone to create his own private work force or his own little army. And I suspect we'll prohibit cloning oneself for mere ego gratification.

Peg Tittle, "We License Plumbers and Pilots—Why Not Parents?" *Seattle Post-Intelligencer*. October 3, 2004. Reproduced by permission of the author.

I imagine we'll enforce some sort of quality control, such that cloned human beings shall not exist in pain or be severely substandard with respect to basic biological or electro-chemical functioning.

And I suspect one will have to apply for a license and satisfy rigorous screening standards. I assume this will include not only meeting certain requirements with regard to the lab and its equipment, but also submitting, and obtaining approval of, a detailed plan regarding the future of the cloned human being; surely we won't allow a scientist to create it and then just leave it in the lab's basement one night when he leaves.

The Risks of Creating Life

The thing is, we can already create human life. Kids do it every day.

It should be illegal to create life, to have kids, in order to have another pair of hands at work in the field or to have more of us than them. It should be illegal to create a John Doe Jr. to carry on the family name and/or business.

And it should be illegal to knowingly create a life that will be spent in pain and/or that will be severely substandard.

As for the screening process, would-be teachers are generally required to study full-time for at least eight months before the state will allow them the responsibility of educating children for six hours a day once the kids become 6 years of age. Many would say we have set the bar too low.

And yet we haven't even set the bar as high—in fact we haven't set a bar at all—for parents. Someone can be responsible not only for a child's education but for virtually everything about the child, for 24 hours a day until that child is 6 years of age—that is, for the duration of its critical, formative years—and he or she doesn't even have to so much as read a pamphlet about child development.

Licensing Parents

As Roger McIntire notes, "We already license pilots, salesmen, scuba divers, plumbers, electricians, teachers, veterinarians, cab drivers, soil testers and television repairmen. . . . Are our TV sets and toilets more important to us than our children?"

"I created someone by accident" should be just as horrific, and just as morally reprehensible, as "I killed someone by accident."

Then again, wait a minute—we have set a bar for parents: adoptive/foster parents. Those would-be parents have to prove their competence. Why do we cling to the irrational belief that biological parents are automatically competent—in the face of overwhelming evidence to the contrary? We have, without justification, a double standard.

One common response to this notion of licensing parents is dismissal with a giggle, as if I'm suggesting the presence of police in the bedroom. But there is no necessary connection between sex (whether or not it occurs in the bedroom) and reproduction (unless, of course, you reject all forms of contraception), so that response indicates an error of overgeneralization. On the other hand, sex can make you a parent only in the biological sense; since I'm proposing that we license both parentage (the biological part of being a parent—the provision of sperm, ovum, and/or uterus) and parenting (the social part of being a parent—the provision of care, very comprehensively defined), the response also indicates an error of undergeneralization.

Creating Life Is No Accident

Another response to licensing parents is a sort of goofy incomprehension, often followed with something like "Well, it's not as if people plan it, you know—usually, it just happens."

Excuse me? It is not possible to create life "by accident"—men don't accidentally ejaculate into vaginas and women don't accidentally catch some ejaculate with their vaginas. (As for failed contraception, there's morning-after contraception and abortion.) "I created someone by accident" should be just as horrific, and just as morally reprehensible, as "I killed someone by accident." (At the very least, such "parents" should be charged with reckless or negligent reproduction.)

Yet another response is dismissal with indignation, because surely such a proposal violates our rights! But do we have the right to replicate ourselves, to create a person? And do we have a right to raise that, or any other, person? There are many good arguments claiming that we don't: for starters, merely having a capability doesn't entail the right to exercise that capability. (Ruth Chadwick has written a good article examining various motives for having kids—she finds them all inadequate as grounds for the right to have them.) There are also many good arguments for claiming that such "rights" are better conceived as responsibilities or even privileges.

One must also be careful about distinguishing between moral rights and legal rights. (Laura Purdy has written an excellent article investigating whether it's immoral to have children when there's a good chance they'll have a serious disease or handicap and David Resnik has written about whether genetic enhancement is immoral or unjust—neither advocates parenting licenses, but their conclusions are nevertheless relevant; for example, if it is immoral to have children with genetic defects, that might serve as a premise supporting parent licensing.)

Double Standards for Parenting

But even if we do have the right to be a parent or to parent, no right is absolute. My rights end where your freedoms begin. The real question is under what conditions do we have those rights and, then, under what conditions are those rights violated. Why, for example, should the right to be a parent depend on the means of becoming a parent? People seeking access to new reproductive technologies are screened for genetic anomalies, infectious diseases and other "high-risk factors"; they must read and understand information about the risks, responsibilities and implications of what they are undertaking; and they must undergo counseling that addresses their values and goals.

Why should children born as a result of assisted insemination or in vitro fertilization be privileged to a higher standard of care in their creation than children born as a result of coitus? These questions about rights are not easy questions to answer, and this particular dismissal of the proposal to license parents reveals gross naiveté.

Yet another dismissal appeals to the difficulty or impossibility of implementing the idea: Who would set the requirements, what would those requirements be, how would they be assessed . . .? Often lurking beneath these concerns is one more: "and I suppose I wouldn't be good enough!" Partly, this is a paper tiger response: The more ridiculous the claim, the easier it is to mock, so people imagine all sorts of complicated and unrealistic policies and procedures that no advocate of parent licenses would ever suggest. (Read Hugh LaFollette, Covell and Howe, and Jack Westman for real proposals.)

Licensing Could Be an Easy Process

And partly, paradoxically, this response reveals a failure of the imagination: Licensing parents could be as simple as when you turn 18, you get the book and study it or take the course, then you take the written test, and the eye test, and if you pass, you get a beginner's license, then you do some hands-on child care for maybe six months under the guidance of a licensed parent, and if you pass that part, you get your license, and if you don't, maybe you try again in a while. Sound familiar? So what's the problem?

Well, those bedrooms and backseats—we could never really control the parentage part. No, not at the moment. But what if we developed a contraceptive vaccination? (But nooo, our little boy scientists, once they'd finished snickering over the name "Dolly," developed Viagra instead.) We could administer the vaccine as a matter of routine, perhaps once puberty is reached. And then, as part of the license, the antidote could be made available.

Most of us have seen broken kids, kids who didn't get what they needed at a critical stage in their development, so they go through life thinking the world owes them something.

To be succinct, the destruction of life is subject to moral and legal examination—so too should be the creation of life, whenever and however it occurs.

One last objection concerns the potential for abuse. Do we really want to give the state this particular power? I have to say, seeing a theocracy coming ever closer, that this is the argument that gives me most pause.

Unwanted Pregnancies Are the Real Threat

I want to point out that just because something will be abused doesn't mean it shouldn't be tried, and I want to point out that our many other licensing policies still exist despite the occasional abuse. But I've read Margaret Atwood's *Handmaid's Tale*. It's chilling. But I've also read the reports of people too drugged out to even know they're pregnant. And it's not a question of which scenario is more likely. One is already happening and has been for quite some time.

Most of us have seen broken kids, kids who didn't get what they needed at a critical stage in their development, so they go through life thinking the world owes them something. And indeed we do. But sadly, tragically, we can't give it to

15

them because that critical window of time has passed: We can't go back and flush from the fetus the chemicals that interfered with its development; we can't go back and provide the baby with the nutrients required for growth; we can't go back and give the child the safety and attention that would have led to a secure personality. Every year, millions of the people we've created so carelessly are being starved, beaten or otherwise traumatized. Thousands die. And that doesn't count the ones still walking around.

2

A Parenting License Would Infringe on Parents' Rights

Albert Mohler

Albert Mohler serves as the president of The Southern Baptist Theological Seminary.

Calls for a parenting license violate the right of parents to raise children. The concept of parental rights has been instrumental in acknowledging the primacy of the family and limiting the power of the government. Advocates of licensing, at core, seek unrestrained state power. Social workers, bureaucrats, and other state-sponsored professionals should not interfere with the human right to raise children.

The last century has witnessed some of the most divisive and confrontational debates in human history—and many of these have focused on the institution of the family. Arguments over marriage, sexuality, reproduction, and justice have placed a giant question mark over the family, subjecting civilization's most basic institution to both social transformation and cultural subversion.

Parental Rights Versus Totalitarian Government

Now, two generations after the contraceptive revolution, the very right of parents to bear and raise children is under renewed attack. The implications of this debate will range far

Albert Mohler, "Should Parents Be Licensed? An Ominous New Debate," *AlbertMohler.com*, April 28, 2005, © All rights reserved, www.AlbertMohler.com. Reproduced by permission.

beyond the question of parental fitness. Inevitably, the real issue is whether the state can or should exert a totalitarian power and influence over the reproductive decisions of its citizens.

While the very question of licensing parents seems like the rerun of a bad movie from the 1960s, the issue has emerged again in connection with the use of new reproductive technologies.

The opening salvo in the debate over licensing parents was fired by philosopher Hugh LaFollette, whose 1980 volume, *Licensing Parents*, set the agenda for formal debate. Published by Princeton University Press, LaFollette's book was ahead of its time. Now, a quarter century later, the debate is almost certain to be renewed.

Evidence of this comes in the form of *Should Parents Be Licensed? Debating the Issues*, edited by Peg Tittle. An ethicist and philosopher, Tittle introduces a lively and interesting series of essays. "Would-be teachers are generally required to study full-time for at least eight months before the state will allow them the responsibility of educating children for six hours a day once they become six years of age. Many would say we have set the bar too low. And yet we haven't even set the bar as high—in fact we haven't set a bar at all—for parents," she asserts.

Clearly, Tittle believes that parents should be required to gain a license in order to bear and raise children. She argues that today's society pays insufficient attention to the needs of children, and fails children specifically by failing to require a minimum standard of expertise from their parents.

Casting Doubt on Parents' Abilities

As Tittle sees it, "having children is not always a good thing." Indeed, she believes that some forms of parenting are simply "immoral." While she obviously has clear cases of parental neglect in mind, she also implies that her understanding of "moral" parenting is tied to a radical liberalism that would see conservative parents—especially conservative *Christian* parents—as dangerous or unfit.

As she explains, "Licensing would also emphatically underscore the immorality of various kinds of parenting, and penalties for parenting without a license or for somehow 'violating' the license might act to deter people from such parenting." Most of the essays in this volume imply that the coercive power of the state must be employed in the licensing process. "To license parents is not just to say that some parenting is immoral," Tittle acknowledges; "rather, it is to go one step further and say that some parenting should be illegal, presumably, but not necessarily, *because* it is immoral."

While the very question of licensing parents seems like the rerun of a bad movie from the 1960s, the issue has emerged again in connection with the use of new reproductive technologies. Questions of access to these technologies, and questions about the morality of reproductive decisions, imply that these questions could—and some would argue *should*—be pushed back to "natural" forms of reproduction as as well.

The belief is that parents own, or at least have natural sovereignty over, their children.

Licensing Advocates Fear Parental Incompetence

LaFollette's essay remains the touchstone of the movement to require licensing for parents. "Our society normally regulates a certain range of activities; it is illegal to perform these activities unless one has received prior permission to do so," LaFollette explains. "We require automobile operators to have licenses. We forbid people from practicing medicine, law, pharmacy, or psychiatry unless they have satisfied certain licensing requirements." Thus, "any activity that is potentially harmful to others and requires certain demonstrated competence for its safe performance, is subject to regulation—that is, it is theoretically desirable that we regulate it."

LaFollette sees parenting as "an activity potentially very harmful to children." He points to instances of parental abuse or neglect and argues that the prevention of such abuse would alone justify a licensing requirement for parents. Added to this, LaFollette argues that some persons lack a minimal competence for parenting. Licensing of parents should be required, "not because state intrusion is inherently judicious and efficacious, but simply because it seems to be the best way to prevent children from being reared by incompetent parents."

Why would this idea be met with resistance? "I suspect the answer is found in a long-held, deeply ingrained attitude toward children, repeatedly reaffirmed in recent court decisions, and present, at least to some degree, in almost all of us," LaFollette suggests. "The belief is that parents own, or at least have natural sovereignty over, their children. It does not matter precisely how this belief is described, since on both views parents legitimately exercise extensive and virtually unlimited control over their children. Others can properly interfere with or criticize parental decisions only in unusual and tightly prescribed circumstances—for example, when parents severely and repeatedly abuse their children. In all other cases, the parents reign supreme."

Parental Rights Limit State Interference

This assertion of parental rights and parental authority is both concise and accurate. Indeed, belief in parental sovereignty over children has been one of the most important means by which the state has acknowledged the primacy of the family, and thus the limits of its own power.

LaFollette rejects this claim out of hand. "This belief is abhorrent and needs to be supplanted with a more child-centered view," he boldly asserts.

Some have taken this argument even further. Margaret Battin, addressing the issue of population control, has suggested that the state might require all persons to use "automatic reversible contraception" that could be reversed only by the authority of the state. The state would allow only those persons it deems qualified for parenting to breed, bear, and raise offspring.

The natural family is under sustained attack from advocates of sexual revolution and agents of state power.

All this leads to a fascinating collision of the claims put forth by various moral philosophers, all working from a basically secular worldview. The idea that the state should require parents to be licensed in order to reproduce flies into direct conflict with Professor John Robertson's assertion that all persons possess a basic right to "procreative liberty." Robertson, who teaches at the University of Texas, would extend this right of procreative liberty to virtually unrestricted access to reproductive technologies and eugenic mechanisms.

Severely Restricting Parenthood

The idea that some decisions to procreate could be characterized as "immoral" requires explanation and elaboration. Some [writers] argue that genetic screening should be used in order to prevent "immoral" births from taking place—births of those deemed unworthy in terms of genetic disease or other defects. Others would extend such concerns to matters of economic viability, arguing that parents should not be allowed to have more children than they can afford. Edgar R. Chasteen, for many years Professor of Sociology and Anthropology at William Jewell College, acknowledges that this would mean limiting the rights of parents. "Laws have been passed that severely restrict the rights of parents over their own children," he notes. "Compulsory school attendance laws, health laws, delinquency laws, housing laws—all have translated parental *rights* into *privileges*. The next logical extension of this process is to make it a privilege to *have* children. Such laws would serve not only to defuse the population bomb, but also to protect firstborn children against the too prolific reproduction of their parents."

Roger McIntire, Professor Emeritus of Psychology at the University of Maryland, calls for a complete reconsideration of "the currently sacred 'right to parent.'" Noting that adoption agencies screen potential parents, he argues that the state should extend this same process to all prospective parents. "Screening and selecting potential parents by no means guarantees that they will in fact be good parents. Yet today we have almost no means of ensuring proper child-rearing methods. The indiscriminate 'right to parent' enables everyone, however ill-equipped, to practice any parental behavior they please." Similarly, Jack Westman, for many years Professor of Psychiatry at the University of Wisconsin Medical School, suggests that parents should be licensed at different stages of a child's life. The requirement of a license would "provide a basis for eligibility for governmental financial aid and supportive services in order to ensure that public funding supports competent and not incompetent parenting." The requirement of a license "would designate parenthood as a privilege for which one is qualified rather than as a right that accompanies the event of childbirth. It would define parenthood realistically as a relationship rather than as a biologically determined state."

Licensing Would Threaten Families

Make no mistake. These calls for parents to be licensed, radical as they may seem, are the logical extension of other arguments that are now taken for granted in many circles. The natural family is under sustained attack from advocates of sexual revolution and agents of state power.

While all morally sensitive persons should be concerned about cases of parental neglect and abuse, the real agenda behind this movement is the replacement of parental authority with the authority of the state. In reality, the right to procreate remains one of the most significant checks against totalitarianism and the otherwise unrestrained power of the state.

The family has already been stripped of many of its responsibilities and protections. Parents are now threatened by state intrusion and bureaucratic interference. An army of various social workers, educational bureaucrats, and therapeutic specialists insists that they know best and that children should be nurtured, disciplined, instructed, and socialized in accordance with their own worldviews. The idea of requiring a license in order to bear children strikes at the very heart of what it means to be human, and what it means to be part of the human family. Watch this debate closely, for it is gaining steam.

3

Parents Should Receive Incentives for Getting Licensed

David Tebaldi

David Tebaldi is the Executive Director of the Massachusetts Foundation for the Humanities.

Marriage is heavily regulated, but, unfortunately, procreation is not. Yet bad parenting causes suffering. High schools should offer classes on parenting skills. While requiring parental licensing might be difficult, future parents should receive economic incentives for getting licensed, and their licenses should be renewed every several years.

I'm wondering why we need a license to get married, but we don't need a license to have kids—especially considering the fact that a bad marriage is easily undone and does no irreparable harm, whereas bad parenting can create a legacy of misery that affects large numbers of innocents and often gets passed on from progeny to progeny.

The English poet Philip Larkin made this point memorably in his poem, *This Be The Verse*:

They f--- you up, your mum and
dad.
They may not mean to, but they
do.
They fill you with the faults they
had

And add some extra, just for you.
But they were f---ed up in their
turn
By fools in old-style hats and coats.
Who half the time were soppy-
stern
And half at one another's throats.
Man hands on misery to man.
It deepens like a coastal shelf.
Get out as early as you can,
And don't have any kids yourself.

Historically, marriage has been pretty heavily regulated in our society. The state tells us who we can marry (or, more accurately, who we cannot marry) and when we can marry. Sixteen states still had anti-miscegenation [interracial marriage] on the books when the Supreme Court finally ruled them unconstitutional in 1967. More recently, the debate over same-sex marriages reminds us that marriage regulations remain a matter of controversy for many Americans and a form of repression for some.

And yet procreation is not regulated at all.

A licensing procedure could easily be established for this purpose, not unlike what is already in place for drivers' licenses.

Encouraging Procreation

There have been state-sponsored attempts to limit procreation—most famously, China's widely misunderstood "one-child" policy. And closer to home, one of the main objectives of schools-based sex education programs in this country is to prevent (or postpone) procreation. In "abstinence only" programs, the goal is to prevent sexual intercourse itself.

More common are state-sponsored efforts to *encourage* procreation. In Italy, where there is growing concern about declining birthrates and the depopulation of many villages, the mayor of Laviano is offering $15,000 baby bonuses to women who give birth and rear their children in this hamlet near Naples. Here in the USA, tax-exemptions for dependent children encourage taxpayers to have children. Anti-abortion policies have the effect of forcing women to have children whether they want them or not.

But there is no state policy or program to determine who should be a parent or, more importantly, to provide basic training in the principles of effective parenting. A licensing procedure could easily be established for this purpose, not unlike what is already in place for drivers' licenses. There would be a written exam, but an interview with a trained psychologist would replace the road test.

Parenting education could be provided by our high schools much as driver's education once was. Indeed, in many public high schools, what used to be called "Home Economics" has morphed into "Marriage and Family Living" and "Nutritional Science." This is good. But these programs tend to be elective rather than required, boys rarely enroll in them, and none of them focus specifically on parenting skills despite the fact that one third of the textbooks used in such courses demonstrate a "pronatalist bias," according to one study.

Licenses Should Have to Be Renewed

Since demands on parents vary greatly as a child matures from infancy to young adulthood, and changing circumstances in the home (e.g., additional children, divorce, etc.) often bring with them a different set of challenges, the parenting license should be renewed every few years.

The fact that there are no effective means of enforcing such license requirements should not dissuade us from promulgating them. Although the state clearly has the right to separate children from parents who are demonstrably unfit, abusive, or neglectful, removing children from homes where the parents are simply unlicensed is not likely to go down well. I would not even support fines for parenting without a license.

But perhaps there could be some practical incentives to comply. The tax-exemption for dependent children, for example, might be limited to licensed parents. If nothing else, the licensing scheme would have a hortatory [beneficial] effect. Even if we cannot compel procreators to be good parents, at the least we can point them in the right direction.

4

Equal Custody Should Be a Human Right for All Parents

Marilyn Gardner

Marilyn Gardner is a staff writer for The Christian Science Monitor.

Divorced parents are increasingly raising their children in shared situations, which give the children nearly equal time with each parent. This arrangement is a change from typical custody arrangements, in which the children live with one parent and only see the other during occasional visits. The parents need to make an effort to ensure this type of situation works, but in the long run, it is most beneficial to the children.

Ever since his parents separated nearly two years ago and then divorced, Danny Hechter has become a master of logistics, dividing his time equally between two homes in suburban Minneapolis. Sunday through Tuesday, the seventh-grader lives with his mother, Lynn Sadoff. From after school on Wednesday until Saturday morning, he stays with his father, Rich Hechter. Saturday noon the three meet for Danny's bowling league. Saturday afternoon and evening are flexible.

"We decided on an exact 50-50 split," says Ms. Sadoff, a hospital publicist. "He had very strong relationships with both of us."

Their arrangement makes them part of a growing band of divorced parents trying to create more equitable arrangements to care for their children. Instead of the traditional approach, in which children live full time with one parent—usually the mother—and spend weekends and some holidays with the other parent, these families split their time. Some choose a 30/70 division, while others prefer a 40/60 or 50/50 sharing.

Staying with both parents is in the child's best interest "only if it's not dangerous, either physically or emotionally for the child."

"More and more men are doing more child rearing during the marriage," says Sharyn Sooho, cofounder of Divorcenet-.com. "As a result, more men are seeking significant parenting roles after divorce, sometimes asking to be primary residential parents."

No national statistics track the number of parents with shared-parenting arrangements. But Daniel Hogan, executive director of Fathers & Families, an advocacy group in Boston, estimates that joint physical custody is awarded 10 to 30 percent of the time, depending on the state.

"It's increasing," he says.

Eleven states have laws that include some presumption of joint physical custody, Mr. Hogan adds. "Only five states say expressly that it's fine to award joint custody even if one party disagrees. It's always at the discretion of the judge to decide if it's in the best interest of the children."

Even those who generally support shared parenting offer a caveat: Staying with both parents is in the child's best interest "only if it's not dangerous, either physically or emotionally for the child," says Mr. Hechter, a family law attorney.

He finds that shared parenting works best when parents reside in close proximity and in the same school district. He and Sadoff live just eight blocks apart, making it easy for Danny to go back and forth.

Successful arrangements also depend on parents' work schedules, their child-rearing skills, and the ages of the children. "The youngest children need one main home base," says Wendy Allen, a psychotherapist in Santa Barbara, Calif., who works with custody issues.

Some critics argue that many children of all ages need one primary home. Lots of shuttling back and forth can be tough, they say. Supporters counter that having a close relationship with both parents outweighs the disadvantage of two homes.

It's definitely harder, but for the children's sake I think it's better that they have both parents in their lives.

Challenges for the Parents

Some divorced parents actually find that the need to maintain regular contact with each other has helped them to forge a good relationship.

"We've been able to look beyond all the ill will and negative feelings that come up," Hechter says. "Both parents have to put their bitterness behind."

That can be a challenge. "If it's an every-other-weekend thing, you're less involved," says Shari, a mother of two on Long Island who asked to be identified only by her first name to protect her sons' privacy. "If they're going to their dad's house this evening, I have to be in touch with him. It's not easy, when the person you're dealing with is the person you made this enormous break with. It's definitely harder, but for the children's sake I think it's better that they have both parents in their lives."

Her teen sons spend 30 percent of the time with their father and 70 percent with her. Calling her former spouse "a good dad and a good ex-husband," she adds, "Considering the circumstances, this was and is a good solution for the children."

Like many offspring who shuttle between two homes, Shari's boys have two sets of certain possessions, as does Sadoff's son, Danny. "We try to have what he needs at both homes—two computers, two sets of research materials," Sadoff says.

"The child must be very well organized, or Mom and Dad must be willing to communicate well and cart stuff back and forth," says Lisa Cohn of Portland, Ore., who was divorced 14 years ago and has remarried. One recent weekend her 17-year-old son, Travis, realized that his soccer gear was at his father's. "His dad met us at the game with his uniform," Ms. Cohn says.

For them, such meetings are amicable. "Over the years, my ex and I have learned to get along very well," Cohn says. The two sit together at school activities and meet with Travis's teachers together. Last month, when Travis went to his first prom, he dressed at his father's house, then went to his mom's so she could see his first tux.

Not all parents can manage such connections. Isolina Ricci, author of "Mom's House, Dad's House for Kids," refutes a common misperception that shared parenting helps to guarantee that the children will be all right. "It doesn't work that way," she says. "Sometimes it is a very conflicted arrangement. That conflict is not a plus for the children."

Dr. Ricci cautions against what she calls parallel parenting. The parents share child rearing, but she likens them to two separate countries. They do not talk to each other and may not have any conversation about the children. Parents with dissimilar lifestyles can leave children equally confused. At one house, they might stay up until 11 p.m. or later with unlimited TV watching and no homework, Ricci says. The other house might be much more structured, with bedtime at 9 o'clock and limited TV.

"When parents have different lifestyles, when they are unwilling to compromise . . . so rules are more consistent, it can be very stressful for children," Ricci says. "It's hard to shift gears."

Although Ricci calls herself a "big supporter" of shared parenting, she cautions that it should not be a catchall for difficult situations. "You can have an old-fashioned parenting arrangement that works just fine."

A Change in Attitudes

Ricci sees a push on some fronts for shared parenting to be the norm. But she emphasizes that parents have an obligation "to take very seriously what it's going to take to be an effective parent. It requires more sophistication, more skill."

Some parents who cannot communicate well in person keep in touch by e-mail. Others coordinate children's schedules on special websites.

Even if parents' relationships are strained, Ms. Sooho urges them to make every effort to be pleasant during pickups and dropoffs. "If the parents are reasonably calm during the transitions, if they are mature and gracious, and say 'Hello, how are you?' [to the other parent], children are usually fine with it."

Mr. Hogan expects that in the short run, passing legislation on shared parenting could be "very tough." As fathers'-rights groups become better organized and more vocal, he says, opponents are also gaining strength. But in the long term, he thinks supporters "will gradually be able to convince the legislatures that shared parenting is a good idea." . . .

Nearly 200 members of Fathers & Families turned out in Boston for a meeting on the issue. "Without the law behind you, you don't really have shared parenting," said Michael Paolino of Hampton, N.H., a participant.

As attitudes toward postdivorce child rearing change, so does the vocabulary. Instead of "visitation schedule," some divorce lawyers and judges now say "parenting schedule," Sooho says. Rather than "custodial and noncustodial parents," they refer to the "primary residential parent" and the "nonresidential parent."

"The words 'custody' and 'visitation' belong to prisons and hospitals," Ricci says. "This may be useful language for the legal system, but not for families."

By whatever name, these complex arrangements produce varied opinions. Neil Gussman of Philadelphia, who was divorced 10 years ago and is remarried, has two teenage daughters who take a positive view. They leave for school from one parent's house and go home to the other.

"I have asked several times over the years if the girls would like a different arrangement, but so far, seeing both parents nearly every day is very important to them," he says.

Shari is cautious: "My sons do get tired of having two of everything," she says. "I don't think we're really going to know how they perceive it until the storms of adolescence pass. But they see, on a regular basis, how their parents put forth the effort to continue this over what is now a very long time."

Looking back over the past eight years, she adds, "It's been an interesting ride. You have to be really committed to it and be willing to do the work to make it happen. But I think it's worth it."

5

Married Couples Have No Right to a Child

William May

William May is the Michael J. McGivney Professor of Moral Theology at the John Paul II Institute for Studies on Marriage and Family at The Catholic University in Washington, D.C.

One of the goals of marriage is to have children. However, if parents are not able to conceive through natural sexual activity, they should not have a right to seek a child through artificial insemination or in vitro fertilization. While many rightly reject the concepts of surrogate mothers and sperm donors, even new methods of procreation should not be used because they involve the participations of persons other than the parents. Only the marital act can bestow the gift—not the right—of life.

Frequently, in discussions about fertility and the use of such techniques as artificial insemination and in vitro fertilization, the claim is made that a married couple has a moral "right" to a child. After all, one of the goods of marriage is the procreation and education of children. Therefore, if a married couple is not able to have a child through normal genital activity, why should they be prevented from using contemporary biological techniques in order to have a child of their own?

The [Catholic] Church, as is well known, teaches that it is morally wrong to generate human life outside the marital act. Many people, both Catholic and non-Catholic, can readily understand why the Church teaches that it is morally bad for a couple to generate human life by inseminating the wife with sperm provided by a man who is not her husband or by inseminating a woman other than the wife with sperm from the husband (i.e., a "surrogate" mother, who would, after the bearing the child, turn it over to the married couple). They recognize that the choice to generate human life in these ways does violence to marriage and to human parenthood and does a serious injustice to the child.

New Reproductive Options Raise New Moral Questions

But many of these same people, Catholic and non-Catholic alike, find the teaching of the Church on the immorality of artificial insemination by a husband and the "simple case" of in vitro fertilization a different matter. In both artificial insemination by the husband and the "simple case" of in vitro fertilization, there is no use of *gametic* [reproductive cell] materials from third parties; the child conceived is genetically the child of husband and wife, who are and will remain its parents. In both these cases there need be no deliberate creation of "excess" human life which will be discarded, frozen, or made the subject of medical research of no benefit to them. In these cases, there need be no intention of intrauterine monitoring (although there could be) with a view of abortion should the child conceived suffer from any abnormality. Nor need there be, in these cases, the use of immoral means (masturbation) to obtain the husband's sperm, since it can be retrieved in morally acceptable ways. In these cases there is, apparently, only the intent to help a couple, despite their physical incapacity (either by reason of the husband's low sperm production or the wife's blocked Fallopian tubes) to have a child with whom they ardently desire to share life and to whom they are willing to give a home. Do not such couples have a "right" to have a child of their own? Why, many people reasonably ask, is it morally bad—indeed a sin, an offense against God Himself—to make use of artificial insemination by the husband and homologous in vitro fertilization in such cases? Is not the Church's position here too rigid, too insensitive to the agonizing plight of involuntarily childless couples who are seeking, by making good use of modern technologies, to realize one of the goods of marriage? Do not married couples in this situation have a right to make use of these methods so that they can have a child of their own?

God, in short, wills that human life be given in the marital embrace of husbands and wives not through the random copulation of fornicators and adulterers.

The Rights of Married Couples

It is definitely true that married men and women have rights (and responsibilities) that nonmarried men and women do not have. They have the right, first of all, to engage in the marital act, that is not simply a genital act between two persons who happen to be married but is an act of interpersonal communion in which they give themselves to one another as husband and wife. In direct contrast to genital sex between an unmarried man and woman which merely joins two individuals who are in principle replaceable, substitutable, disposable, the marital act unites two persons who have made one another absolutely irreplaceable and nonsubstitutable by giving themselves to one another in marriage.

In addition, husbands and wives, by giving themselves to one another in marriage, have capacitated themselves, as St. Augustine put it, "to receive life lovingly, to nourish it humanely, and to educate it religiously," i.e., in the love and service of God. Unmarried men and women to the contrary have not so capacitated themselves. God, in short, wills that human life be given in the marital embrace of husbands and wives not through the random copulation of fornicators and adulterers.

Husbands and wives, thus, have a "right" to the marital act and to care for life conceived through this act, but they do not have a "right" to a child. A child is not a thing to which husbands and wives have a right. It is not a product that, by its nature, is necessarily inferior to its producers, rather a child, like its parents. And this is the moral problem with the laboratory generation of human life, including artificial insemination by the husband and the "simple case" of in vitro fertilization.

Children Are Gifts, Not Products

When a child comes to be in and through the marital act, it is not a product of their act but is "a gift supervening on and giving permanent embodiment to" the marital act itself (Catholic Bishops [of England and Wales] Committee on Bioethical Issues . . .). When human life comes to be through the marital act, we say quite properly that the spouses are "begetting or procreating," they are not "making" anything. The life they receive is "begotten, not made."

But when human life comes to be as a result of various types of homologous fertilization, it is the end product of a series of actions undertaken by different persons. The spouses "produce" the gametic cells that others use in order to make the end product, in this case, a child.

Husbands and wives have no "right" to make a child.

In such a procedure, the child comes to be, not as a gift crowning the marital act, "but rather in the manner of a product of a making and, typically, as the end product of a process managed and carried out by persons other than his parents"

(Catholic Bishops of England and Wales Committee on Bioethical Issues), the life generated is "made," not "begotten."

Begotten, Not Made

But, as noted already, a human child is a person equal in dignity to its parents, not a product or a thing. A child, therefore, ought not to be treated as if it were a product.

In the Nicene-Constantinople Creed that we say at Mass every Sunday, we profess that God's Eternal Word was "begotten, not made." Human beings, as being made in God's image and likeness, are, as it were, the "created words," brothers and sisters of God's Eternal and Uncreated Word, that manifest from the depths of God's personal love for every human person. Thus human beings, the "created words" of God, like his Eternal and Uncreated Word, ought to be "begotten, not made." Husbands and wives have no "right" to make a child. They have the right to give themselves to one another in the marital act and, in and through this act, to receive the gift of life.

6

The Joy of Parenting Should Be Considered a Privilege

Mary Beth McCauley

Mary Beth McCauley won the Religion Newswriters Association Supple Award for Writer of the Year in 2000 for work in The Philadelphia Inquirer.

Parenthood, especially in families where both parents work outside the home, seems to be increasingly difficult. It's time for parents to rediscover parenting, to make do with less money, and to devote time to caring for children. Being able to serve the family has its own satisfactions and rewards. Instead of seeing it as a chore, mothers and fathers should view parenthood as a satisfying, if work-intensive, privilege.

A friend of mine recently brought his elderly mother to live with him. He has a big job and a long day, but one of his favorite things is bringing her a piece of pie in the evening. It's even better if she accepts a little ice cream on it. I can just see her—with her blue eyes twinkling. But the greater pleasure is his.

I know this from caring for my children. I know how good it feels to comfort an infant simply by offering milk, to make a teenager's day better by standing there listening. As with much of mothering, none of this is special, nothing worth mentioning. The greater pleasure is mine. Which is why I'm puzzled by the never-ending debate over child care.

Parenting Is a Privilege

A study released in July by the National Institute of Child Health and Human Development, for example, compared certain behaviors of children in home care with those in day care. In another study, also released in July, researchers at the University of Minnesota's Institute of Child Development compared levels of stress hormones in children in home care versus day care.

The opinionizing spawned by such data seems always to miss the big picture while reaching the same conclusion: Men should do more at home so that women can do less, freeing them to do something better elsewhere. This approach—reducing parenting into pieces of data, repackaging it as single-serving chores, and assigning it out equally—mischaracterizes as lesser work what many see as the privilege of caring for a family.

Some find life actually better with one spouse at home, even if it means selling the second car, keeping the clothes until they fray, and dining three nights in a row on the supermarket special of the week.

Cathy Hetznecker, mother of two, of Havertown, Pa., understands why. "My life consists of very, very minute details of somebody else's life, details no one outside my house cares about," she said. Her research project for the day, she notes for illustration, might be finding something that baby Willa will eat. But fortunately for Willa, currently fussy about her food, there is someone who is willing to take on the challenge.

All work can be drudgery; any can be meaningful. The ideal of diaper-changing parity makes no sense. It ignores the fact that division of labor works well for many families. And, really, what breadwinner trying to get a flight out of Detroit at 2 A.M. wouldn't rather have that middle-of-the-night feeding? What is it about a marketing meeting that makes it inherently more palatable than chopping tomatoes, listening to Puccini, and laying out the cloth napkins? Isn't each spouse—on a good day, at least—simply doing whatever is needed to help create the life they both want?

Less Can Mean More

Where is the love? Sometimes, at-home parenthood seems unaffordable. After all, parts of our culture consider parents neglectful if they nix that fifth trip to Disney World. But some find life actually better with one spouse at home, even if it means selling the second car, keeping the clothes until they fray, and dining three nights in a row on the supermarket special of the week.

"We live simply," says at-home mother Amy Horn, of Merion, Pa. "We like imparting to our children that we should not always be striving for the next thing." She and her husband opted off the bigger, busier bandwagon after her whirlwind tour through graduate school. "It just didn't feel like that was the way life should be."

Her husband, like many men, initially was taken aback by her desire to stay home, but quickly recovered. He is grateful, at day's end, for a meal on the table and his family nearby, and she is grateful that she can make that happen. Even despite his being diagnosed with cancer two years ago, she rejects the notion that a career will make a woman less vulnerable in the event of widowhood or divorce. "I can't walk around each day planning for every event that could happen," she says.

Susan Hamilton, of Drexel Hill, Pa., admits to being "micromanaged" by the needs of her brood—a baby, 3-year-old twins, and a 4-year-old. She times her shower to coincide with a certain kiddie TV show, and runs out for milk in the tiny sliver of time between morning and afternoon naps.

Enjoying the Small Gifts

But she doesn't consider her life a sacrifice: "I'm part of what they're doing—the good things and the bad things. Here, I can root out what I don't like and put in what I like."

She and her husband plan to get away together for a whole day this fall. "I think we're doing all right," she says.

For one of my children, the sure cure for anything that ails her is to curl up with me on the sofa, Regis on the TV. Our family's pace often allows me to indulge her, and I try to make sure I do.

This (my own personal research) never fails to convince me that the greater joy—the serving of the pie—is always mine.

7

Men Should Have the Right to Refuse Parenthood

Anna Smajdor

Anna Smajdor is a lecturer in Ethics at the University of East Anglia.

Only women are allowed to insist on an abortion. While men can't force women either to have an abortion or give birth to a child, they are forced to accept either parenthood or abortion, without any legal say in the matter. Even after birth, mothers still have the right to give the child up for adoption—men don't. Yet both partners should have the right to refuse parenthood, and should be allowed to choose whether or not they want to share in the legal, social, and financial care of the child.

On 10 April 2007, Natallie Evans lost the final stage of a four year legal battle for the right to implant embryos created with her eggs and the sperm of her former partner. Ms Evans had been diagnosed with cancer, and treatment necessitated the removal of her ovaries, leaving her sterile. Creating and storing embryos would, it was hoped, keep the possibility of motherhood open to her.

However, Ms Evans' hopes were shattered when her relationship broke down and her partner, Howard Johnston, withdrew his consent for the embryos to be used. Since the consent of both parties is required for fertility treatment or even for ongoing storage of embryos, it seemed that Ms Evans would have to forego her dream of parenthood. But she was unwilling to submit to the loss of her embryos without a fight, hence the protracted legal struggle which culminated in the European Court of Human Rights' rejection of Ms Evans' case.

Parenthood Involves Many Aspects

Many people, while sympathetic to Ms Evans' plight, felt that the court had come to the right conclusion. After all, the consent protocols are clear and were accepted by both parties at the time the embryos were created. But while in the eyes of the law the correct decision may have been reached, the case raises some interesting questions. The implication was that people should not be forced to become parents, all other things being equal. Is this an acceptable conclusion? And is it consistent with other legal and social assumptions?

The presumed right to abortion is sometimes construed as stemming from a right not to be a parent.

To answer this question, we need firstly to examine the concept of parenthood. I suggest that parenthood is best understood not as inhering solely in genetic ties. Rather, it is a bundle of concepts which may include some or all of the following: being part of a causal chain that brings about the creation of a child; having the intention to procreate; undergoing gestation and childbirth; acquiring legal rights and responsibilities; sharing genetic links; nurturing and rearing.

We may be justified in believing that some of these types of parenthood should not be forced on unwilling people. Forcing people to undergo gestation and birth against their will seems clearly unacceptable. But perhaps the 'right' not to be a parent in the genetic sense has been mistakenly extrapolated from the idea that enforced gestational parenthood is a moral wrong.

The presumed right to abortion is sometimes construed as stemming from a right not to be a parent. But to whom does this right apply? Men are not allowed to force women to undergo abortions, so does this mean that the right applies only to women? Margaret Brazier has suggested that fundamental human rights 'must be gender-neutral'. If this were true, then surely a right not to be a parent ought to apply to both sexes.

In fact, men undergo enforced genetic parenthood all the time, and society scarcely registers the fact.

Protecting Autonomy Over One's Body

However, abortion cannot simply be described as an exercise of the right not to be a parent in the genetic sense. If a woman has been impregnated with an embryo that has no genetic link with her, does this mean she has no choice whether or not to continue with the pregnancy? Surely the important fact is that the embryo is inside her body, not that it does or does not share her genes.

This is a vital fact to remember, since what we are protecting here is people's autonomy over their bodies. It is perfectly coherent for respect for autonomy to be afforded to men and women alike. On the other hand, the right not to be a genetic parent, when it conflicts with physical concerns, seems either to come with so many constraints as to be almost worthless, or to lead to unpalatable conclusions. (E.g. that a pregnant woman can be coerced by those who are the genetic parents of the embryos she is carrying.)

Maintaining autonomy over one's body is of the utmost importance. Women have fought long and hard for the right to do so. We must not conflate this with the altogether separate—and lesser—issue of enforced genetic parenthood.

The harms involved in physical coercion and enforced parenthood are very evident. However, the harms involved in enforced genetic parenthood are far less clear. In fact, men undergo enforced genetic parenthood all the time, and society scarcely registers the fact. A man whose partner is pregnant cannot demand she has an abortion. But we could feasibly allow men to sign a waiver stating that they do not consent to the birth of the child, and that they wish to play no part in the child's life or upkeep.

It seems highly discriminatory that the partners of fertile women have no rights whatsoever in this respect. A man whose partner has become pregnant without his desire or knowledge has the legal and financial obligations of parenthood thrust upon him, whereas men whose partners are infertile are accorded the right to veto the entire reproductive enterprise.

Pregnant Without the Father's Consent

This being the case, perhaps we should be more sympathetic to men whose partners are pregnant without their consent. Mr Johnston is simply one of many, many men in the UK who go partway toward parenthood and then get cold feet. There is a degree of moral opprobrium associated with reluctant fathers. We are encouraged to see them as being selfish, feckless and irresponsible. But taking the risk of unprotected sex and then deciding one doesn't want to be a father is arguably no more culpable than creating embryos and then changing one's mind. The latter is perhaps worse, as it involves reneging on an agreement and causing grief to one's partner.

The asymmetry of the law with respect to fathers and mothers, whether fertile or not, needs to be straightened out. Even after the ties of gestation and birth are over, mothers are not forced to accept the further legal and financial obligations of parenthood. They can choose to give their children up for adoption. Men do not have this right. They are utterly at the whim of their partners' choices. In this environment, men's rights are very much constrained compared to those of

women. And this constraint extends far beyond what is justified by the mother's physical connection with the child.

It is my contention that this injustice should be remedied. Not by respecting men's or women's 'right' not to be parents, but by affording men and women the same rights in terms of choosing not to assume legal, social or financial responsibility for the child.

In the context of this far greater injustice to men in the UK, I have limited sympathy with Mr Johnston. He, along with other men and women, should have the opportunity to state his refusal to fulfill the function of a social parent, and this should be recognisable in law. If this were possible (and we allow it in the case of gamete donors), it would be hard to see what further harm could come to Mr Johnston purely from the knowledge that a child might be born with some of his genes. Certainly any such harm is far harder to identify or quantify than the harms of enforced physical, legal or financial parenthood.

8

Families Should Not Have More Than Two Children

Dalton Conley

Dalton Conley is director of New York University's Center for Advanced Social Science Research and author of The Pecking Order: Which Siblings Succeed and Why.

The current policy to provide tax breaks for families with many children is misguided. Having many children not only hurts America's competitiveness in the global economy, but also hinders the development and education of these children. When a family has more than two children, the later-born children suffer educational setbacks. Furthermore, the U.S. economy needs fewer, more educated people to stay competitive. The United States government should revise tax policy to discourage large families. This would not amount to more state control, but merely reverse how American policies already influence family size.

The U.S. government encourages families to have children, as many of them as possible. Child tax credits, child-care tax deductions, and family leave policies all reward parents with big broods. The pro-child policies are based partly on romantic notions about mom, family, and apple pie, but they also have a rational goal: We subsidize kids so that our next generation of workers is ready to win in the global economy.

Quality Trumps Quantity

Problem is, these two goals—more kids and better prepared kids—are at odds. If we really care about kids' welfare and accomplishment, the United States should scrap policies that encourage parents to have lots of children. As my recent research shows, having more than two children is tantamount to handicapping their chances for academic, and thus economic, success. In this information economy, what we ought to be doing through the tax code is making it easier for parents to ensure the quality of their first one or two children, not stimulating quantity. Pro-fertility tax policy is an outdated notion from an industrial era when we needed bodies to fill manufacturing plants. Today we need fewer, highly skilled kids who will compete with our rivals in math and science.

The third child is . . . less likely to receive parental financial investment in his or her education. . . .

It's long been known that kids from large families perform worse in school, but it has been impossible to explain why. That's because research about the relationship between family size and children's educational achievement has been plagued by a nagging issue: Large families tend to be different from small families on a number of fronts—religiosity, commitment to education, orientation to the future, maybe even intelligence level. So it has been hard to assess the impact of the number of children in a family as distinct from these other differences. (Maybe Johnny can't read because he has unintelligent parents, not because he is the sixth of nine kids.) After all, with all due respect to Chairman Mao, we can't randomly assign parents to have different numbers of offspring for the purposes of social experimentation—that is, to find out if additional kids handicap offspring.

Parents Desire Children of Each Sex

Here's where my research comes in. I deploy a natural experiment: I examine which sexes parents get for their first two children—a seemingly random event. The key is that families with two kids of the same sex are 17 percent more likely to go on and have a third than those with two kids of the opposite sex. As it turns out, no matter what most people say on surveys (or when their kids pop out), many parents desire at least one of each kind. So my research strategy boils down to the following: comparing children from families in which the first two were of the same sex ("treatment group") to those in which the first two were of the opposite sex ("control group") in order to see who fares better educationally. In other words, while only some of the variation in who goes on to have a third child is accounted for by the sex mix (that 17 percent), that variation is "pure"—that is, unbiased by all the other factors that determine family size and determine achievement—since it is a result of the random event of the sex mix. Its lack of bias is bolstered by the fact that it does not matter which sex the first two are—either way, parents are more likely to go on to have additional kids in search of a complete set.

We have to confront the possibility that a more powerful educational (and antipoverty) policy is a tax structure that acts as a disincentive to have more children.

With the addition of the third child, firstborns don't appear to suffer on the educational front. But middle-borns are severely hurt by the addition of another mouth to feed: His parents are 25 percent less likely to send him to private school, and he is several times more likely to be held back a grade. The third child is also less likely to receive parental financial investment in his or her education and can suffer from elevated risk of academic failure. Evidently, only firstborns get off scot-free.

A New Policy Proposal: Smaller Is Better

The reasons that additional siblings hamper the intellectual growth of children (and particularly middle-borns) are fairly obvious—parental resources are a fixed pie, and children do better when they get more attention (and money). The conclusions to be drawn are more controversial. For example, we always talk about the goal of raising test scores and the overall "intellectual" or "human" capital of our population to fit the needs of the new information economy (and to compete with other nations in math and science), yet our tax policy does the exact opposite: It gives tax credits for additional kids. We have to confront the possibility that a more powerful educational (and antipoverty) policy is a tax structure that acts as a disincentive to have more children. Research has long shown that family background is a lot more important than school conditions in predicting academic success or failure. Just about the most controllable aspect of family background is how many kids are in that family. So it stands to reason that a more effective education policy may be to provide economic disincentives to large families.

Perhaps a suitable compromise would be to have a declining tax credit—granting a big subsidy for the first kid, a bit less for the second, then cutting back to nothing (not unlike the current system for the Earned Income Tax Credit). Such an adjusted tax credit (and associated deductions) makes economic sense since the addition of the first kid is the most expensive. It makes educational sense, and last of all, it makes common sense. After all, do we really want to subsidize kid No. 9?

Reversing Existing Tax Policies

Such a fertility-unfriendly policy would put us at odds with European nations that are desperately trying to stimulate population growth by increasing the tax incentives to have more kids; but then again, if we can't find common ground with the Europeans in foreign policy, what should make domestic policy any different? (Unlike most of Europe, we have a steady influx of immigrants to sustain population growth.)

More important, the antibrood tax policies would anger those on both sides of the political aisle here in the United States. Religious conservatives—who see procreation as a divine imperative—may take offense at the notion that the government would not do all it could to facilitate this goal. Similarly, many on the left will protest that such a policy is class-biased, allowing rich people who would be less fazed by the additional expenses to have as many children as they please while leaving poor people to feel the extra pinch. Americans of all political stripes might take offense at the notion of the government getting involved in the sacred sphere of family life. But the truth is that we already are meddling with family fertility through our tax code. We're just not acknowledging it, and, furthermore, we're doing it the wrong way. We need honest discussion about the trade-offs between child quantity and quality.

9

Too Many Children May Be Bad for the Planet

Gregory M. Lamb

Gregory M. Lamb is a staff writer for The Christian Science Monitor.

The idea that too many people are on Earth is not a politically popular one, but it is something that needs to be discussed. Some feel that the world population has already reached a critical point and is harming the environment. Many also note that people in more industrialized countries use more resources and have a greater effect on the planet than people from less developed countries. The solution may not be government limits on the number of children families can have, but steps need to be taken to reduce population growth.

A re there too many people on Earth?

That question is rarely raised today, in part because it conjures up the possibility of governments intruding into the most private and profound decision a couple can make. In a worst-case scenario, authorities could impose discriminatory policies that would limit births based on such criteria as race, ethnic origin, cultural background, religion, or gender.

But with huge, vexing questions such as food security, poverty, energy supplies, environmental degradation, and climate change facing humanity, some are asking whether aggressive measures to control population growth should be on the public agenda.

Politicians generally stay clear of suggesting population-control policies, recognizing the deep-seated concerns they raise. President Obama did not mention the issue as part of his campaign last fall. But the new Obama administration has promised to take a fresh look at solutions to energy and environmental challenges and has brought in a new slate of scientific advisers. The United States remains the only developed country without an official population policy.

Might the new administration dare to raise the idea?

Some ... argue that even today's population is too large to maintain without ravaging the environment and creating an inhospitable planet.

"You've got to get a president who's got the guts to say, 'Patriotic Americans stop at two [children],'" says Paul Ehrlich, a professor of population studies at Stanford University. "That if you care about your children and grandchildren, we should have a smaller population in the future, not larger." Professor Ehrlich wrote the groundbreaking 1968 book *The Population Bomb*, which predicted disastrous effects from unchecked population growth.

Can Population Growth Be Sustained?

Earth's population is about 6.8 billion people today, or four times the population of a century ago. Even though birth rates are lower than during the 1960s and '70s, the world is adding 75 million to 80 million people per year and is expected to peak at more than 9 billion by midcentury—far too many, say some population experts.

Whether this growth can be sustained and still provide a decent living standard for people is itself controversial. Some, including Ehrlich and Alan Weisman, the author of the best-selling book *The World Without Us*, argue that even today's population is too large to maintain without ravaging the environment and creating an inhospitable planet.

How much would today's population have to shrink to become sustainable? "I don't think anybody knows," Mr. Weisman says. "All I know is, 'less is better.'"

Weisman's book imagines a world in which humans are extinct and suggests that nature could bounce back relatively quickly from the burden placed on it by its billions of human inhabitants.

Everyone living in an industrialized nation puts a much heavier burden on the environment than does someone living in, say, Asia or Africa.

Demographers calculate that if suddenly every family on earth limited itself to one child, by 2150 the world's population would be 1.6 billion, exactly what it was at the beginning of the 20th century.

He's not arguing that that's a perfect number of humans. But "it would create a lot more space for [other] organisms to live . . . a much healthier ecosystem for us all," he says.

Lifestyles are a Bigger Issue

Ehrlich and Weisman agree with critics who say population alone isn't the issue. Lifestyles in developed countries in North America and Europe consume a lot of resources. Everyone living in an industrialized nation puts a much heavier burden on the environment than does someone living in, say, Asia or Africa. Though family sizes in the developed world are smaller, the number of households hasn't shrunk commensurately.

"It's actually the number of households—and not the number of people—that has a bigger impact on the environment," says Matthew Connelly, a professor of history at Columbia University in New York and the author of *Fatal Misconception: The Struggle to Control World Population.*

"This is not a population crisis," Professor Connelly argues. "The crisis is us, the consumption patterns of the wealthiest people in the world. That's what's unsustainable." The problem in trying to control populations "is that we don't know how to do it," he says. "We don't have a good theory to explain, much less predict, why people have babies and why they have as many as they do."

China's strict one-child-per-family policy, established 30 years ago, has cut its population growth significantly. But it has also created a huge gender imbalance, as families have chosen male children over female, he says.

"There's a long history of governments trying to make it illegal for parents to have large families," Connelly says. "China is just the most notorious example." But, he asks, "Is that the kind of country we'd like to live in, where the government could make it illegal to choose the number of children we have?"

Doom-and-gloomers Assume Technology is Static

Those arguing that a calamity awaits if population isn't reduced are looking at the past and trying to project it into the future, says Ted Nordhaus, an environmentalist and coauthor with Michael Shellenberger of *Breakthrough: From the Death of Environmentalism to the Politics of Possibility.*

"They assume that technology and resources are static," Mr. Nordhaus says, and that breakthroughs and discoveries that could dramatically improve living conditions on earth won't be found.

"The greatest antidote to rapidly growing population is prosperity and development," Nordhaus says. "As people become more prosperous, birth rates decline. . . . It's an economic development challenge, not a population challenge."

But that doesn't mean that we need to just sit back and do nothing. "We can't take a laissez-faire approach to this," he says. "We can't just assume technology advancement will happen as quickly as we would like it to. There are all kinds of things we need to do to invest in productivity improvement."

Despite the fears of some, rising living standards in the developing world don't mean that the environment will be devastated in the process, he says. The idea that Chinese and Indians will all be driving around in Humvees and flying in private jets is "not true," he says.

The concept of some environmentalists that humans are somehow an intruder or "a scourge on the earth" disturbing an otherwise harmonious nature, needs to be challenged, Nordhaus says. "The reality is that nature is neither stable nor harmonious," he says. "We're as natural as anything else, and a world with us is as natural as a world without us."

Everyone born in 1965 or earlier and still alive has seen human numbers more than double from 3.3 billion in 1965 to 6.8 billion in 2009.

Short of government limits on family size, both advocates and opponents of population control agree that many other useful steps can be taken that may lead to reduced population growth. Among the most crucial are better education, economic opportunities, and access to contraceptive and reproductive health care services for women in developing countries with high birth rates.

As economist Robert Cassen put it in 1994, "Virtually everything that needs doing from a population point of view needs doing anyway."

Emerging Trends in Global Population

What effects will world population growth have by the mid-21st century? Joel Cohen, head of the Laboratory of Populations at Rockefeller University and Columbia University, makes the following points:

- In 1950 the less-developed (poorer) regions of the world had roughly twice the population of the more developed (richer) ones. By 2050 the ratio will exceed 6 to 1.

- Human numbers currently increase by 75 million to 80 million people annually, the equivalent of adding another United States to the world about every four years.

- At present, the average woman bears nearly twice as many children (2.8) in poor countries as in rich countries (1.6 children per woman).

- Some 51 countries or areas will lose population between now and 2050. Germany is expected to drop from 83 million to 79 million people, Italy from 58 million to 51 million, Japan from 128 million to 112 million and the Russian Federation from 143 million to 112 million.

- If recent trends continue as projected to 2050, virtually all of the world's population growth will be in urban areas.

- Everyone born in 1965 or earlier and still alive has seen human numbers more than double from 3.3 billion in 1965 to 6.8 billion in 2009.

- The peak population growth rate ever reached, about 2.1 percent a year, occurred between 1965 and 1970. Human population never grew with such speed before the 20th century and is likely never to grow with such speed again.

10

Mentally Disabled People Face Bias in Parenting Rights

Ian Mulgrew

Ian Mulgrew is a Canadian journalist and senior reporter for The Vancouver Sun. He has authored three books.

Barbara Gamble is mildly mentally handicapped. Canadian social services agencies, deeming her unfit to parent, have taken her five children from her at their birth. Yet she is pregnant again and hoping to keep her child and raise it with the father, also mentally handicapped. She wants to prove that disabled couples can make good parents. Gamble's history, however, is one of drugs and homelessness, and a psychologist judged her incapable of parenting.

Barbara Gamble rubs her distended belly and sighs with despair. The pregnant 27-year-old is about to deliver her sixth child, not counting the set of twins she lost. But it isn't the birthing process that has her worried.

Government workers have seized every child the moment it is born: a baby girl (Breanna) was apprehended in Alberta and four other children, two girls (Chyanne and Laura) and two boys (Dean and Jake), have been taken into care in British Columbia.

"None of them," Gamble laments. "I've not been allowed to breast-feed any of them."

Losing Her Children

The routine always has been the same—shortly after delivery, a social worker arrives, flips her a card, declares the child is being apprehended and leaves with the baby.

"It is horrific," Gamble says. "All the labour, carrying and delivering a baby, and then they rip it from your arms. It's cruel."

She is considered unfit to parent primarily because she isn't as smart as everyone else and there aren't enough support services to bridge the gap.

Gamble scores between 63 and 71 on the standard IQ test, "mildly mentally handicapped," according to the official reports on her case.

The way she tells it, she didn't really know "about this whole pregnancy thing, or how to get pregnant, what it's all about. So I went and I ended up getting pregnant."

Gamble has never seen the five kids together, only those born in B.C. [British Columbia], whose dad is her current partner, 30-year-old Vince Kinney. The only time she saw them together, she said, was roughly a year ago.

"They have all been apprehended right at birth," Gamble repeats in a flat monotone. "It's been very emotionally hard to deal with. I don't receive any information, pictures, letters, updates, nothing at all."

Canada stopped sterilizing handicapped women four decades ago, but lawyer Mark Hargrave says the government has effectively achieved the same goal by seizing Gamble's children at birth.

"This is worse than forced sterilization because you carry the baby for nine months with the knowledge they're going to seize it," Hargrave says. "I don't know how she and Vince do it. They've never had a night with a baby. It is unbelievable. It is unbelievable to me that our society would permit that."

Unable to Cope

Gamble and Kinney are two of the tragic faces of 21st century poverty, a couple often unable to cope with the demands made on them because of their low intellectual capacity and concomitant [resulting] lack of judgment.

The way she tells it, she didn't really know "about this whole pregnancy thing, or how to get pregnant, what it's all about. So I went and I ended up getting pregnant."

Gamble was born in Lethbridge, Alta [Alberta], but her mother moved to Maple Ridge shortly afterwards.

She left school in 1999 to live with a male classmate in Quesnel, B.C.

"I went to live with him because I didn't want to live with my family any more," says Gamble. "I have felt that way since I was eight years old. I didn't want to be in the system or anything, I just wanted to be on my own, independently."

Gamble moved to Surrey, B.C., but her family warned social workers that they believed her incapable of caring for an infant and that the man she was with was abusive. Nevertheless, Gamble fled to Alberta and stayed with his family in January 2000, hoping to avoid having her baby seized.

It didn't work.

When Breanna was born, Alberta Social Services took her into custody. They obtained a permanent guardianship order that December. Gamble went into a tailspin.

Spiraling into Crime and Drug Use

She returned to B.C., lived on the streets, experimented with drugs, became pregnant with twins in 2002, and lost them. It was during this period she was picked up brandishing a screwdriver and charged with uttering threats.

"When I first met Vince (in April 2003) because I had no place safe to go, I stayed with him and he (helped) get me onto disability," she explained.

She currently receives $906 [Cdn] a month from the B.C. Ministry of Human Resources.

Kinney told her doctors he was unable to father children, so she was surprised a month after they met to find herself pregnant.

The moment the social workers learned at the end of August 2003 that Gamble was pregnant, the couple realized they had a problem.

Chyanne was born on Feb. 8, 2004, and was immediately seized by social workers who alleged, among other things, that Gamble and the newborn had tested positive for heroin. That was false.

"We went down to community services and we tried to figure out what services could be offered to us to help us to be a family," Gamble said. "We didn't quite get why they apprehended Chyanne at first, because I didn't use drugs."

In psychological reports, Gamble is described as "emotionally immature, needy and lacking in insight. She is distrusting, egocentric, depressive, highly anxious, and reactive."

Kinney and Gamble were assigned a family outreach worker, but they bristled and soured at being told they weren't able to parent as well as anyone else.

In the midst of the legal battle over Chyanne, Gamble became pregnant again. That fall they underwent a parental capacity assessment that was conducted by Dr. Michael Elterman.

A Crushing Assessment

Although they were defensive and participated grudgingly, Elterman's opinion is the foundation of the ministry's decision-making. He did not think Kinney and Gamble were capable parents.

Dean was born on Jan. 26, 2005. He, too, was seized at birth.

In psychological reports, Gamble is described as "emotionally immature, needy and lacking in insight. She is distrusting, egocentric, depressive, highly anxious, and reactive."

Awaiting the arrival and the loss of another child, Gamble says she is emotionally wrecked.

So why continue to get pregnant?

"I'm willing to do whatever it takes to be allowed to have a family and if this is what it takes, then so be it . . ."

11

The Intellectually Disabled Can Be Good Parents

Andrew Freeway

Andrew Freeway is a writer for Disability World.

Mentally disabled couples can raise normal families, despite the social stigma and society's misgivings about them. Often, disabled people are seen as asexual and treated like second class citizens, yet examples show that children of disabled people thrive in their families. Some couples might need a helping hand from social services, but a disability doesn't keep them from being excellent parents.

William Westveer and his wife Irma have 2 healthy boys, and both [parents] have an intellectual disability. Westveer, who is the director of the Dutch advocacy organization LFB, equivalent to People First [advocacy group run by developmentally disabled persons], has very strong opinions about forced anti-conception and other meddlesome interventions.

"Irma and I decided to have kids. So we went to our general practitioner to have check ups and ask some questions. Irma's mother has MS [multiple sclerosis] and her father has emphysema of the lung. And my mum died of cancer, just like her brother. And my father also suffered from lung emphysema. And above all, I have a sister and a brother with Down syndrome. So Irma and I really wanted to know what our odds were for getting a disabled child", says Westveer.

But the doctor reassured them that Down syndrome was not hereditary. And cancer could be everybody's fate and he advised them to have a check up at the gynecologist. He also stated that their right to have children should not be hindered by the fact that they had an intellectual disability.

Most intellectually disabled people are either seen as asexual persons or as people who are not able to make autonomous decisions on sexuality and reproduction.

Working as a Team

"We thought this over very carefully and read a lot of books on the subject. But finally, after consulting the doctors who were very supportive, we decided to go for it," Westveer commented.

The Dutch Health Council recently published a study called 'Contraception for People With an Intellectual Disability'. This study is meant to give doctors something to consult when counseling intellectually disabled people with questions concerning contraception and reproduction. At the moment most physicians do not know which way to turn when confronted with these questions. This situation can be attributed to a lack of knowledge and the lack of a social debate, according to the Council. Most intellectually disabled people are either seen as asexual persons or as people who are not able to make autonomous decisions on sexuality and reproduction. Therefore deliberate decisions on these matters are seldom taken by those involved. And the result of this indecisive behavior is very often either an unwanted pregnancy or a very frustrated person.

According to the Council it is evident that some intellectual[ly] disabled persons are not fit to raise a child. In those cases it is wise to prevent a pregnancy. And, the Council report continues, if a disabled person is unable to give informed

65

consent, then forced contraception should be considered. But the law says that interventions are only allowed to prevent serious damage to a person's health and having a baby can hardly be seen as such a hazard. General practitioners, gynecologists and urologists should work closely together with those physicians who are trained to take care of people with an intellectual disability in order to assess a person's ability to raise a child, says the Council, and an IQ of 60 could be considered as the minimum.

A disability should not keep you from living independently or having children.

"Both our kids are healthy; Joeri is seven and Brian is four and has asthma. He almost suffocated because the doctor made a mistake. It was not our own doctor but a substitute doctor. Brian became ill during one evening and this substitute doctor gave him some medicine for the flu. But we knew better and wanted to go to the hospital. But the doctor did not find that necessary. Of course we ignored him and went directly to the pediatrician who had had Brian's asthma under control since birth. Brian was admitted to an intensive care unit and stayed there for a couple of days. When I confronted the substitute doctor with this outcome, he became very angry and said that we were mad [crazy] to go to the hospital".

Making Wise Parenting Decisions

"We are getting 1.5 hour professional support every week. They have checked us out how we were handling the children. For example, did we punish the children, how often and how did we punish them? And what kind of arrangements we had made for sleeping and eating. Joeri for instance is a handful as far as eating is concerned. He does not like meat. So we had to find ways to convince him that emptying his plate was worthwhile. If he does not want to finish his dinner we tell him that we will have fries the next day but that we will re-heat his dinner. Wow, what an incentive! And if they are really annoying us, we tell them to sit on the staircase and rethink their behavior. Irma and I decided from the beginning that we would never spank our children. Beating only makes children aggressive. It is much better to take away their privileges like locking away a puzzle if they cannot stop arguing and telling them they can get it back if they behave.

"Disturbed parents of disabled children are our biggest stumbling block. They are very much against our organization. We should not become too bright. But it is not about being sweet or not. It is about the rights of people. A disability should not keep you from living independently or having children. At our headquarters troublesome news is coming in about the way institutions are forcing people to have a contraceptive injection. If you do not accept this way of birth control you are not admitted to the institution. But as far as we are concerned all institutions may close tomorrow. That way we will save a lot of money not spent on care managers and institutional merges. Cause that is all what they do: merge, merge, merge!"

Disabled People Need Time and Respect

"Let me make myself clear: I do not think that all people should have children. My own sister for instance wanted to have a child a couple of years ago. The institution called me and told me that my sister wanted to stop the contraceptive injection and that it might be better if she was sterilized. Instead I invited my sister to stay with us for a fortnight and suggested that she could practice with our newborn Joeri. After a couple of days she decided that she did not want children. Taking care of them was too much a burden, she thought. And when I asked what she wanted to do when she was having sex with her boyfriend, she said she preferred to be sterilized. When my sister came back in the institution she informed the staff of her decision. Later that day they called me asking what I had done to convince her. I told them I did not convince her; I just gave her the opportunity to consider her options and find out what she really wanted. She never had the opportunity to see and practice what life with a child would be. It was just a question of time and respect, that's all. But time and respect are the most lacking ingredients in institutions. Having a law that makes it possible to enforce contraceptive injections or sterilization is not necessary. Just close down all those institutions, give people their own budget so they are able to buy personal support and a lot of things will go much better."

12

The Cognitively Impaired Should Not Be Forcibly Sterilized

Damon W. Root

Damon W. Root is an associate editor of Reason *magazine. Root is a graduate of Columbia University and writes on legal affairs and constitutional history.*

Women with disabilities should not be sterilized against their will. Forced sterilization is not a solution to the social problems of crime, poverty, and disease, despite the burdens that these problems place on society. The practice of forced sterilization was common in the early 20th century and is a standout example of an abuse of government power.

In his startling new book *Three Generations, No Imbeciles,* Georgia State University law professor Paul A. Lombardo looks at the Supreme Court's notorious 1927 decision in *Buck v. Bell,* which upheld a Virginia law permitting the forced sterilization of the "feebleminded and socially inadequate."

At the center of the case was a young woman named Carrie Buck. She had been raped and impregnated by the nephew of her foster mother, then committed to a state institution by her foster parents, where she was sterilized. In his majority opinion, Justice Oliver Wendell Holmes dismissed Buck, her mother, and her daughter as "mental defectives" and declared, "Three generations of imbeciles are enough."

Associate Editor [of *Reason* Magazine] Damon Root spoke with Paul A. Lombardo in September [2008].

Q: What happened to the girl at the center of the case?

A: Carrie Buck was a girl who was about 17 years old. When the story begins she finds herself pregnant without a husband. She gives birth in the same year that the Virginia legislature passed a law that calls for sterilization of people who are so-called socially inadequate, which includes people who are in institutions like the Virginia Colony for the Epileptic and the Feeble-Minded. Carrie Buck gets sent to that colony, which is an asylum for people with various kinds of disabilities. She gets sent there because she is declared to be a moral defective.

Q: Her lawyer, Irving Whitehead, has a relationship with this institution, right?

A: One of the great ironies is that the building in which Carrie Buck is sterilized has a plaque on the front of it—it's still there—which has her lawyer's name on it as a member of the board of directors of the Colony in its earliest years. He advises and votes in favor of sterilization.

He essentially throws the case. He doesn't present any evidence on her behalf, no witnesses at all. In the book, I think I present good evidence that the fix was in. By any measure, whether it's today or the measure of 100 years ago, he stands out in terms of his unethical behavior.

A Radical Definition of Government Power

Q: Justice Holmes' ruling shows incredible deference to the state.

A: It's the most blunt kind of statism. If we can draft you into the Army, he suggests, then we ought to be able to sterilize you. We execute criminals; why can't we sterilize these people in the asylums? He says, well, we've endorsed the idea of vaccinating people in the time of smallpox epidemics. If we can vaccinate them, we ought to be able to sterilize them. He

says it's not too much of a leap from doing a vaccination to cutting the fallopian tubes, as if these two things were somehow equivalent. So Holmes does really break new ground in terms of a radical definition of state power.

When governments start deciding who can have children, they almost always botch it.

Q: Does the idea of eugenics still have any appeal?

A: Most people, if given the option, would vote to have less of a burden of social welfare costs and lower taxes. That's a popular idea for all of us. The argument that's made during the Buck case is that you get there by doing away with the people who generate those costs.

The real problem is that we all still feel that way today. Not that we want to be Nazis, and not that we want to re-enact eugenic laws. But we all still are looking for solutions to social problems and ways of managing the inevitable social burdens of crime, poverty, and disease. The hope that we can find those solutions is of course still with us—and should be, I think—but what we use as a means toward those is of course the question. I argue in this book that one of the things we shouldn't use is the power of government through coercive medicine. When governments start deciding who can have children, they almost always botch it.

13

Physically Disabled Women Have the Right to Maternity

Joanna Karpasea-Jones

Joanna Karpasea-Jones is the author of the books Vaccination: Everything You Should Know About Your Child's Jabs and More, *and* Breast Milk: A Natural Immunisation. *Karpasea-Jones also set up the Vaccination Awareness Network UK in 1997. The Network deals with vaccination issues for concerned parents.*

Physically disabled women should not shy away from becoming mothers. They are just as qualified as the able-bodied to take care of their children. They may be required to do tasks such as changing diapers in public places differently than able-bodied mothers, but that does not make them wrong. The children of the disabled also do not necessarily have to inherit their parents' physical disabilities, which can be a big fear for the parents.

When I fell in love and moved in with my soul mate, I was 16 years old—in itself a big problem for my parents. But I also have cerebral palsy, a result of my premature birth, and my partner has hereditary motor and sensory neuropathy, a condition in which messages to his brain are "scrambled," causing muscle wastage, bone deformations that require surgery, and decreased sensation of pain, heat, and cold. Any children we would have would have a 50/50 chance of inheriting the disability from him. Clearly, we had some thinking to do.

I assumed that we wouldn't take this risk, and suggested to my partner that I be artificially inseminated with sperm from a donor. He was totally against the idea, saying that he didn't want to see me pregnant by another man—even if he was the daddy, the child would not be biologically "his." I understood this. Nor did adoption seem a choice, as then I would never be pregnant or give birth—a thought that was heartbreaking to me. And in Britain in the 1990s, it was difficult to adopt if you had any kind of physical health problem. Even today, being only slightly overweight disqualifies you from adopting.

We decided to team up with a genetics charity and volunteer to write genetics coursework for General Certificate of Secondary Education (GSE) students. (GSE is basically equivalent to a high school diploma in the US.) Perhaps these kids, then only two or three years younger than I, could shed some light on what they would do.

We presented our case in a fact file for students of sociology and ethics, and a few weeks later were inundated with letters that the teachers had passed on to us—heartfelt letters full of wobbly writing and spelling errors, saying that yes, we should go for it and have a baby, because we were disabled but were still glad to be alive. These children were so spirited and impassioned that, reading all their letters, I had tears in my eyes.

Then, when I was 17, we went to a genetics counseling session, where I learned everything I could about genes and my partner's disability. We were told that any affected child would have the condition at a similar level of severity as my partner. Well, he could walk, drive a car, carry heavy things, and do nearly everything an able person could do. That clinched it—we decided to go ahead. Nearly everyone in our families was disabled anyway: me, my partner, his brother and father, my aunt and uncle. If the child was affected, she certainly wouldn't feel the odd one out. Normality is subjective; to us, disability was normal.

The Pregnancy and Birth

My pregnancy caused a sensation. My own mother told me we had been irresponsible to take such a risk and asked me to get an abortion. She said that, with my cerebral palsy, I would never be able to care for the baby, and it would end up on the UK's "at risk" register, which lists children who are either being harmed or are at risk of being harmed (and whose families are then closely monitored by the child-protective services). My partner's mother said that I wouldn't be able to carry a baby to term, and that I'd need a cesarean section because I was too weak to give birth. Obviously, kids are more open-minded than the adults who raise them.

The plastic cribs were positioned too high for me to be able to lift my baby out. I solved this problem by putting the crib on the floor and sitting in a chair so I could reach down to pick her up.

I felt pleased when I found myself 11 days overdue without so much as a twinge. That'll show them, I thought. I was already six centimeters dilated before we left for the hospital.

The hospital staff seemed to have no idea about mobility impairment when they brought out stirrups for the pushing stage and expected me to use them.

"I have CP. My legs don't move like that."

"Well, how will you give birth, then?" asked the midwife.

I told her I was going to do it sitting upright, and she'd just have to hold my legs. And that's what we did. I pushed my first child into this world like most other women, after being in the delivery room for only six hours—not bad for a first birth.

Parenting in a Different, Flexible Way

The postnatal experience was even more interesting. They had only two bathtubs on the ward, neither of which I could get into; that meant that, for my two days there, I had to rinse down at a sink. Mothers were expected to fetch their own breakfast, and I couldn't carry plates without a tea trolley, so by the time I'd gotten a midwife to help me, most of the food was gone. The abled mothers had first pickings. The plastic cribs were positioned too high for me to be able to lift my baby out. I solved this problem by putting the crib on the floor and sitting in a chair so I could reach down to pick her up. My balance was too poor to carry her as the other mums did, so I had a pram [baby transport] on the ward with me and wheeled her around in that.

The midwives followed me around incessantly, saying they wouldn't let me go home until they'd seen me change a nappy [British term for diaper], and asking such questions as, "How will you take her up the stairs?" "I won't!" I told them. The baby would sleep downstairs until my husband got home. I was perplexed that they could think of only one way of doing things. In my opinion, the true disability is a lack of flexibility.

After we'd returned home, the health visitor—the nurse who came to weigh the baby and give me parenting advice—asked more questions than I did. She seemed to be learning more about me as a disabled parent than I was about parenting.

The day my baby took her first steps was an emotional one for me—I hadn't walked till I was nearly five, and here she was, walking at only 15 months.

Of course, when we used cloth nappies, when we decided not to vaccinate our child, when we set up the Vaccination Awareness Network UK, and when we enlisted a homeopath, we felt others were judging us as disabled parents who had no idea how to be parents. It's hard enough to be holistic when the whole world seems to be drowning in controlled crying, vaccinations, disposable diapers, and tacky advertising; it's doubly challenging for a disabled teenage mum to raise her child in a spiritual way without people thinking it's because she's just plain different.

Going out and about with my daughter was an adventure, especially as the public toilets for the disabled were also the baby-changing rooms. Often, when I needed to go, there'd be a queue of mums backed up outside, waiting to change their own babies, and I'd be rushing to finish and leave and not hold up the queue. As for changing my own baby, the table was too high for me to lift her onto it, and even if I'd managed, she could have rolled off and fractured her skull. All changing rooms, therefore, were unusable to me. Instead, I would lower the back on her stroller and change her in that.

The day my baby took her first steps was an emotional one for me—I hadn't walked till I was nearly five, and here she was, walking at only 15 months. She'd wobble, reach out, grasp my leg for support, and I would just smile down at her and tell her there was no sense learning from Momma—I couldn't do it any better than she could!

When our daughter turned two, we got the wonderful news: She wasn't disabled in any way at all. We went on to have three more girls; none of them has inherited her father's disability.

14

Gay Couples Should Not Be Barred from Raising Children

Alan Hirsch and Brad Sears

Brad Sears is executive director of the Williams Institute on Sexual Orientation Law and Public Policy at the University of California at Los Angeles School of Law Alan Hirsch is a senior consultant for the Institute.

Arguments against same-sex marriage are often based on religious principles or on prejudice. However, studies concerning gay and lesbian parenting show that there is no discernible difference between children raised by opposite-sex or same-sex couples. Any fears that children with homosexual parents suffer in these families are groundless, and society should drop its discrimination against same-sex parents.

[In summer 2003], the Supreme Court struck down laws criminalizing sodomy, stating that a majority's moral views cannot justify an infringement on individual rights. In dissent, Justice Antonin Scalia bemoaned the fact that the court's decision "leaves on pretty shaky grounds state laws limiting marriage." If morality cannot justify a ban on gay sexual intimacy, Scalia asked, "what justification could there possibly be for denying ... marriage to homosexual couples?"

Good question.

Most objections to same-sex marriage seem to be rooted in religious faith or prejudice and defy proof or disproof.

Alan Hirsch and Brad Sears, "Straight-Out Truth on Gay Parents," *Los Angeles Times*, April 4, 2004. Copyright © 2004 Los Angeles Times. Reproduced by permission of the authors.

However, opponents of same-sex marriage do invoke one line of reasoning that can be confirmed or refuted by evidence.

That argument concerns children, and rests on two related contentions: First, unlike heterosexual couples, gay couples generally do not raise children and therefore do not need the benefits of marriage. Second, to the extent that gays do raise children, they do the children harm.

Gay Couples Raise Children

As it happens, the best available evidence shows that both arguments rest on fantasies and false stereotypes.

The proclivity to raise children is neither automatic among mixed-gender couples nor off-limits to same-sex couples. The 2000 U.S. Census showed that in California, half of married couples and one-third of gay couples are raising children. (The latter figure is 28% if limited to one's "own" children—a census term that includes biological, step and adopted children—but climbs to 32% when unrelated children, such as foster kids, are included.) More than 70,000 children in California are being raised by gay couples.

What about the notion that children raised by gay parents suffer as a result? This too turns out to be unsubstantiated.

No differences were found in the toy, game, activity, dress or friendship preferences of boys or girls with gay parents compared with those with heterosexual parents, nor any differences in sexual attraction or self-identification as gay.

More Similarities Than Differences

The American Academy of Pediatrics' (AAP) Committee on Psychosocial Aspects of Child and Family Health issued a report in 2002, the most recent comprehensive review of gay-parenting studies. It found no meaningful differences between children raised by gay parents and those raised by heterosexual parents.

The committee reviewed scientific literature encompassing three broad sets of studies. The first set assessed the attitudes, behavior and adjustments of lesbian and gay parents and found, according to the AAP report, "more similarities than differences in the parenting styles and attitudes of gay and nongay fathers." Likewise, the research showed that lesbian mothers scored the same as heterosexual mothers in "self-esteem, psychologic adjustment and attitudes toward child rearing."

The second set of studies looked at the gender identity and sexual orientation of children raised by gay parents. The committee report found that none of the several hundred children studied evinced gender identity confusion, wished to be of the other sex or consistently engaged in cross-gender behavior. No differences were found in the toy, game, activity, dress or friendship preferences of boys or girls with gay parents compared with those with heterosexual parents, nor any differences in sexual attraction or self-identification as gay.

The third research area discussed in the report covers children's emotional and social development. These studies have primarily compared children raised by lesbians who are divorced with children of divorced heterosexual mothers. The only significant difference between children raised by same-sex couples and children raised by heterosexual couples is that the former feel freer to explore occupations and behaviors unhampered by traditional gender roles. No differences have been found in personality measures, peer group relationships, self-esteem, behavioral difficulties, academic success and quality of family relationships. The studies suggest only one meaningful difference: Children of lesbian parents are "more tolerant of diversity and more nurturing toward younger children than children whose parents are heterosexual."

The American Academy of Pediatrics report is the most prestigious of its kind, but it is not the only one. Most reviews of the social science research reach the same conclusion: The proposition that children suffer when raised by gay parents is without basis. Indeed, some evidence suggests that the only significant difference between children raised by same-sex couples and children raised by heterosexual couples is that the former feel freer to explore occupations and behaviors un-hampered by traditional gender roles—a good thing, perhaps.

Most objective observers find no reason to accept the no-tion that children need protection from gay parents.

To be sure, gay-parenting studies to date are limited, and some scholars criticize them because their samples are too small or because they aren't representative of all gay parents. Also, a few studies purport to establish negative characteristics of children raised by gay parents, but they tend to be dis-counted because they are associated with anti-gay researchers and organizations.

While gay parenting needs further study, this much is clear: Most objective observers find no reason to accept the notion that children need protection from gay parents.

And that means it's time to drop the canard [deceptive story] that gay couples do not raise children or do not raise them well.

15

Gay Fathers Cherish the Privilege to Care For Their Children

Julian Sanchez

Julian Sanchez is a contributing editor for Reason. *Sanchez joined the magazine in 2003 and writes on topics such as technology, privacy, and sexual politics.*

Gay fathers can be just as effective as heterosexual parents in raising children in a loving home. Many states are considering or already have implemented measures to prevent gay men from adopting a child, even if the child in question already lives with the gay couple as a foster child. Often these measures don't explicitly prevent adoptions by gay parents, but work to make the process more difficult than necessary or serve as a condemnation of the gay lifestyle. Studies have shown that these actions are excessive, as children of gay couples are as likely to be successful as children of heterosexual couples.

Wayne LaRue Smith had never been so happy to be called *bitch.*

About two months earlier, Smith and his partner, Dan Skahen, had taken in a 3-year-old foster child we'll call Charlie. The boy had emerged from the caseworker's car redolent of stale cigarette smoke, hair matted and tangled, barely able to walk, and, except for the occasional raspy cry, stone silent. "We think," whispered the caseworker, leaning in, "he's retarded."

Week after week, Smith recalls, Charlie refused to say anything. Then one day, as Smith was trying to prevent the boy from climbing around on the furniture, Charlie uttered the first word Smith had heard escape his lips: "Bitch!" Nonplussed at the vocabulary ("He didn't learn that language from us!" Smith says), Smith was nevertheless delighted that the child had said *something.* His silence broken, Charlie pressed his tiny fists to his hips and added "Asshole!" before scampering away. Within weeks he was speaking in complete—and more polite—sentences.

Charlie wasn't retarded. He had simply withdrawn from a world that until then hadn't given him much reason to be engaged with it. That sort of history, sadly, is shared by many of the children who find their way into the nation's foster care systems, which included half a million kids when the Department of Health and Human Services last counted, with some 126,000 available for adoption. At the end of fiscal year 2003, 30,000 of those children were in Florida, more than in any other state except New York and California, with more than 5,000 available for adoption.

Charlie lucked out with Skahen and Smith. As of last April, Florida could not even account for the whereabouts of more than 500 children nominally in its custody. Every few years, the state's papers dutifully report an especially tragic case of a child rescued from a bad home only to be deposited by the state into some fresh hell. One such child is Yusimil Herrera, who after being moved dozens of times from one foster home to another, homes in which she was beaten and sexually abused, won a famous lawsuit against the state in 1999. (The verdict was later overturned, and Herrera settled her claim.) She now stands accused of murdering her own young daughter.

Charlie was one of 23 foster children Skahen and Smith have taken in since 1999. The two boys they're now looking after have been with them for years, and Smith and Skahen would like to adopt them, to spare them the prospect of who-knows-how-many desultory transitions from foster family to foster family.

Right now only Florida explicitly prohibits any gay person from adopting, but just six states and the District of Columbia explicitly allow *adoptions by homosexuals.*

Laws and Restrictions

But in Florida, thanks to orange juice pitchwoman Anita Bryant's 1977 "Save the Children" campaign, the Department of Children and Families' adoption forms carry a pair of "yes" and "no" check boxes—page 5, part II, section G—below the statements "I am a homosexual" and "I am a bisexual." Check "yes" to either and you're ineligible to adopt. The law, as its sponsor explained shortly after it passed, was meant to alert gays that "we wish you'd go back into the closet."

Thanks to this law, Skahen and Smith can log on to the Department of Children and Families' Web site and find a photograph and description of their older boy, on offer to any nice heterosexual couple who'd like to take him away from his family.

Right now only Florida explicitly prohibits any gay person from adopting, but just six states and the District of Columbia explicitly *allow* adoptions by homosexuals. In most cases there's no formal policy, and several states either are known for family judges disinclined to grant homosexuals custody or have indirect statutory barriers to gay parenting. Nebraska banned gay foster parenting in 1995. Mississippi and Utah allow only married couples to adopt, a restriction geared in both cases to exclude gay couples. Just under half of U.S. states permit "second-parent adoption," which grants parental rights to both members of an unmarried couple, in at least some jurisdictions. And more restrictions may be on the way. . . .

In 2004 the U.S. Supreme Court refused to hear an appeal of a lower court decision upholding Florida's ban on gay adoption. The challenge was brought by the American Civil Liberties Union on behalf of Smith, Skahen, and other gay parents. Among the plaintiffs were Steve Lofton and Roger Croteau, who care for five children born with HIV. Three of the kids have been with the couple since infancy. . . .

State legislatures are now pushing to erect a variety of legal barriers to gay couples seeking to raise kids. Carrie Evans, state legislative lawyer for the Human Rights Campaign, a gay advocacy group, has tracked state legislation on gay parenting since 2000. "This year has been the worst," says Evans. "Usually we have a few, but I've never seen this many in one year." Just four months into 2005, lawmakers in seven states—Alabama, Arkansas, Indiana, Oregon, Tennessee, Texas, and Virginia—had introduced bills that would restrict the parenting rights of gay couples and individuals. . . .

Lesbian and gay parents are as likely as heterosexual parents to provide supportive and healthy environments for their children.

The Phantom Menace

The mantra that "children need a mother and a father" has acquired a patina of conventional wisdom through frequent repetition. Yet there is little evidence that children raised by gay couples fare worse than other children.

Gay rights opponents such as Family Research Institute chief Paul Cameron and the Family Research Council's Timothy Dailey are fond of arguing that gay men are disproportionately likely to molest children—a potent charge rejected by the serious social scientists who have directly investigated it. Large-scale studies of molestation victims have repeatedly found that abusers overwhelmingly were either heterosexual in adult relationships or lacked any sexual response to adults.

Noting that about a third of molestation cases involve male adults targeting male children, Dailey and Cameron insist those adults must, by definition, be homosexual. Since homosexual men make up a far smaller proportion of the general population, Dailey reasons, gay men must be disproportionately likely to abuse children.

The problem with this view is that psychologists generally regard pedophilia an orientation of its own. Men who molest boys are not necessarily—indeed, are almost never—"gay" in the colloquial sense. Even if one accepts a definition that calls such men "homosexual," the fact remains that there is little overlap between that group and men who pursue romantic relationships with other adult men, the relevant comparison group for gay adoption.

Most child welfare professionals don't see things Dailey and Cameron's way. After reviewing the available data in 2002, the American Academy of Pediatrics endorsed second-parent adoption rights for gay couples. A resolution passed by the American Psychological Association in 2004 declared that there was "no scientific evidence that parenting effectiveness is related to parental sexual orientation: lesbian and gay parents are as likely as heterosexual parents to provide supportive and healthy environments for their children." It also noted that "the children of lesbian and gay parents are as likely as those of heterosexual parents to flourish." . . .

Family Values

On a drizzly weekend at the end of April, some 250 gay parents, prospective parents, and their kids gathered at Sligo Middle School in Silver Spring, Maryland, for a day-long Family Pride Coalition conference on gay parenting. Standing under a scrolling rainbow LED marquee announcing "Congratulations, Honor Roll Students," Cayo Gamber, a writing professor at George Washington University, surveyed the day's dense program and quipped: "It would be wonderful if straight people came to parenting with this kind of scrutiny.... For us it's a choice, not an accident or a destiny."

At a breakout workshop on adoption, a few dozen participants studied the details of that choice. Panelists related their experiences adopting through private agencies, through foster care, and from the shrinking number of foreign countries open to gay parents. They recounted spending tens of thousands of dollars, waiting anxious months, sitting through lengthy and intrusive interviews and "home studies," and filling out mountains of paperwork in a process one likened to "buying a house and applying to grad school simultaneously."

The hearts of conservatives would, one might think, be warmed by such a group. They feel the universal human need for family as deeply and acutely as anyone and are unusually determined to make committed parenting a central part of their lives.

Those behind the burgeoning assault on gay parenting would have us believe these people are a menace to the children they would take in. And had any of them visited Sligo Middle School that afternoon, they surely would have heard their share of complaints from the children and teenagers in attendance: complaints about homophobic teachers, about classmates whose peers and parents have taught them to use gay as an epithet. Concerned conservatives might ask those kids: Are those complaints a sign there's something wrong with your gay families, or with the broader culture?

Better still, they could visit Florida and ask a child in foster care which makes him feel more threatened: the thought of being raised by homosexuals, or the prospect of an indefinite number of years spent passing through an indefinite number of homes. They could ask whether "family values" are best served by attempting to marginalize gay couples who raise families, by "protecting" abused or sick children from people who want to give them a home, by forcing parents to worry whether they'll have the legal authority to bring their kids to the hospital in an emergency. They could ask Charlie.

Organizations to Contact

The editors have compiled the following list of organizations concerned with the issues debated in this book. The descriptions are derived from materials provided by the organizations. All have publications or information available for interested readers. The list was compiled on the date of publication of the present volume; the information provided here may change. Be aware that many organizations take several weeks or longer to respond to inquiries, so allow as much time as possible.

AARP Foundation Grandparent Information Center (GIC)
601 E Street NW, Washington, DC   20049
Phone: (202) 434-2296 • Fax: (202) 434-6474
e-mail: gic@aarp.org
Web site: //www.aarp.org/life/grandparents

The AARP GIC is a program of the American Association of Retired Persons (AARP). The GIC is an outreach service for grandparents in traditional and non-traditional family roles, including grandparents raising grandchildren and step-grandparents. It offers information and referrals regarding the visitation rights of grandparents, parenting grandchildren, and positively influencing grandchildren's lives. The GIC Web site includes articles and a database of local support services.

American Academy of Child & Adolescent
Psychiatry (AACAP)
3615 Wisconsin Avenue NW, Washington, DC   20016-3007
(202) 966-7300 • Fax: (202) 966-2891
Web site: //www.aacap.org

The mission of the AACAP, a professional organization of child and adolescent psychiatrists, is to promote mentally healthy children, adolescents, and families through research, training, advocacy, prevention, comprehensive diagnosis and treatment, peer support, and collaboration. The AACAP publishes the *Journal of the American Academy of Child and Adolescent Psychiatry*.

American Counseling Association (ACA)
5999 Stevenson Avenue, Alexandria, VA 22304
(703) 823-0252 • Fax: (800) 473-2329
Web site://www.counseling.org

The American Counseling Association is a non-profit professional and educational organization that provides leadership training, publications, continuing education opportunities, and advocacy services to its members. ACA helped set professional and ethical standards for the counseling profession, working toward strengthening the accreditation, licensure, and national certification of counselors.

American Foster Care Resources, Inc. (AFCR)
PO Box 271, King George, VA 22485
(540) 775-7410 • Fax: (540) 775-3271
e-mail: afcr@afcr.com
Web site://www.afcr.com

AFCR is a publisher of resource materials for foster care providers, the children in care and their families, and placing agencies' staff and administration. AFCR's publications cover such topics as AD/HD, discipline, sexual abuse, independent living, recruitment, and support groups.

Big Brothers Big Sisters of America (BBBSA)
230 North 13th Street, Philadelphia, PA 19107-1538
(215) 567-7000 • Fax: (215) 567-0394
e-mail: bbbsa@aol.com
Web site://www.bbbsa.org

Big Brothers Big Sisters is a federation of agencies enabling adult volunteers, through a matching and mentoring program, to serve as friends, mentors, and role models for school-aged children and teens. The BBBSA agencies provide professional casework support and locally focused programs. Many of the agencies also provide programs for children and families in the areas of substance abuse, sexual abuse, teen pregnancy, juvenile delinquency, and children with disabilities.

The Center for Bioethics and Human Dignity

Trinity International University
Deerfield, IL   60015
   USA
(847) 317-8180 • Fax: (847) 317-8101
e-mail: info@cbhd.org
Web site: http://cbhd.org

The Center seeks to engage the issues of bioethics using the tools of rigorous research, conceptual analysis, charitable critique, leading-edge publication, and effective teaching. Recognizing that biblical values have exercised a profound influence on Western culture, the Center explores the potential contribution of such values as part of its work. Articles are published on its Web site.

Center for Family Connections (CFFC)

350 Cambridge Street, Cambridge, MA   02141
(617) 547-0909 • Fax: (617) 497-5952
e-mail: cffc@kinnect.org
Web site: //www.kinnect.org

The goal of the Center for Family Connections (CFFC) is to serve individuals and families touched by adoption, foster care, kinship, and guardianship as well as other complex blended families by offering training, education, consultation, advocacy, and clinical treatment. CFFC publishes the *Kids Newsletter.*

Childhelp USA

15757 North 78th Street, Scottsdale, AZ   85260
(480) 922-8212 • Fax: (480) 922-7061
Web site: //www.childhelpusa.org

Childhelp USA is dedicated to meeting the physical, emotional, educational, and spiritual needs of abused and ne-

Grandparents Rights Organization (GRO)
100 West Long Lake Road, Bloomfield Hills, MI   48304
(248) 646-7177 • Fax: (248) 646-9722
e-mail: RSVLaw@aol.com
Web site: //www.grandparentsrights.org

The Grandparents Rights Organization is a national nonprofit volunteer organization founded in 1984. GRO's purpose is to educate and support grandparents and grandchildren and to advocate for grandparents' desire to continue the grandparent–grandchild relationship, which may be threatened by the death or divorce of the parents or by family fighting.

Planned Parenthood Federation of America (PPFA)
434 West 33rd Street, New York, NY   10001
(212) 541-7800 • Fax: (212) 245-1845
www.plannedparenthood.org

Planned Parenthood Federation of America is a health care provider, educator, advocate, and global partner helping similar organizations around the world. Planned Parenthood delivers health care services, sex education, and sexual health information to millions of women, men, and young people. Articles and fact sheets about a large variety of health topics can be found on its Web site.

glected children by focusing its efforts and resources in th eas of treatment, prevention, and research. The organiz publishes news articles and stories on its web site.

Circle of Parents

200 South Michigan Avenue 17th Floor
Chicago, IL 60604-2404
(312) 663-3520 • Fax: (312) 939-8962
Web site://www.circleofparents.org

The mission of the Circle of Parents is to prevent child a and neglect and to strengthen families through friendly, portive, mutual self-help parent support groups. It publ tip sheets online.

Family Support America (FSA)

205 West Randolph Street, Chicago, IL 60606
(312) 338-0900 • Fax: (312) 338-1522
Website://www.familysupportamerica.org

Family Support America (FSA) works to strengthen and power families and communities so that they can foster optimal development of children, youth, and family mem FSA provides technical assistance, training and education, addresses a variety of topics online.

Family and Youth Services Bureau (FYSB)

National Clearinghouse on Families and Youth
Silver Spring, MD 20911-3505
(301) 608-8098 • Fax: (301) 608-8721
Web site: //www.acf.hhs.gov/programs/fysb

The Family and Youth Services Bureau is part of the U.S. partment of Heath and Human Services, Administration Children and Families. FYSB is dedicated to supporting you people and strengthening families by providing runaway a homeless youth service grants to local communities. The l reau has also created a support network that includes a i tional hotline and referral system for runaway and homel youth, training, onsite consultations, and the dissemination information.

Bibliography

Books

David Archard   *Children: Rights and Childhood, 2nd ed.* London: Routledge, 2004.

————, and Colin Macleod, eds.   *The Moral and Political Status of Children: New Essays.* Oxford: Oxford University Press, 2002.

Michael Austin   *Conceptions of Parenthood: Ethics and the Family.* Aldershot, UK: Ashgate Publishing, 2007.

Denise Brodey   *The Elephant in the Playroom: Ordinary Parents Write Intimately and Honestly About the Extraordinary Highs and Heartbreaking Lows of Raising Kids with Special Needs.* New York: Hudson Street Press, 2007.

Allen Buchanan et al.   *From Chance to Choice: Genetics and Justice.* Cambridge: Cambridge University Press, 2000.

Naomi Cahn and Joan Hollinger   *Families by Law: An Adoption Reader.* New York: New York University Press, 2004.

D. Merilee Clunis and G. Dorsey Green   *The Lesbian Parenting Book, 2nd ed.* Berkeley, CA: Seal Press, 2003.

Ronald Cole-Turner, ed.   *Beyond Cloning: Religion and the Remaking of Humanity.* Harrisburg, PA: Trinity Press International, 2001.

Paul Donahue   *Parenting Without Fear: Letting Go of Worry and Focusing on What Really Matters.* New York: St. Martin's, 2007.

Debra Evans   *Without Moral Limits: Women, Reproduction, and Medical Technology, Updated ed.* Wheaton, IL: Crossway Books, 2000.

Sally Geis and Donald Messer   *The Befuddled Stork: Helping Persons of Faith Debate Beginning-of-Life Issues.* Nashville, TN: Abingdon Press, 2000.

Susan Gelman   *The Essential Child*, New York: Oxford University Press, 2003.

Deborah Glazer and Jack Drescher   *Gay and Lesbian Parenting.* Philadelphia: Haworth Press, 2001

John Harris and Soren Holm, eds.   *The Future of Human Reproduction: Ethics, Choice, and Regulation.* New York: Oxford University Press, 2000.

Marcia Inhorn and Frank van Balen, eds.   *Infertility around the Globe: New Thinking on Childlessness, Gender, and Reproductive Technologies.* Berkeley: University of California Press, 2002.

David Kennedy   *The Well of Being: Childhood, Subjectivity, and Education.* Albany: SUNY Press, 2006.

John Kilner, Paige Cunningham and W. David Hager, eds.   *The Reproduction Revolution: A Christian Appraisal of Sexuality, Reproductive Technologies, and the Family.* Grand Rapids: Eerdmans, 2000.

| Glenn McGee | *The Perfect Baby: Parenthood in the New World of Cloning and Genetics.* Lanham, MD: Rowman & Littlefield, 2000. |

| Oliver O'Donovan | *Begotten or Made? Human Procreation and Medical Technique,* Oxford: Oxford University Press, 1984. Reprinted 2002. |

| Lainie Friedman Ross | *Children, Families, and Health Care Decision Making.* Oxford: Clarendon Press, 2002. |

| Maura Ryan | *Ethics and Economics of Assisted Reproduction: The Cost of Longing.* Washington, DC: Georgetown University Press, 2003. |

| Brent Waters and Ronald Cole-Turner | *God and the Embryo: Religious Voices on Stem Cells and Cloning.* Washington, DC: Georgetown University Press, 2003. |

| Jess Wells, ed. | *Home Fronts: Controversies in Nontraditional Parenting.* New York: Alyson Books, 2000. |

Periodicals

| Michael Austin | "The Failure of Biological Accounts of Parenthood," *The Journal of Value Inquiry,* 2004. |

| Tim Bayne | "Gamete Donation and Parental Responsibility," *Journal of Applied Philosophy,* 2003. |

————, and
Avery Kolers

"Toward a Pluralistic Account of Parenthood," *Bioethics*, 2003.

Christopher
Belshaw

"More Lives, Better Lives", *Ethical Theory and Moral Practice*, 2003.

Marcia Bok

"Families Tied," *The American Prospect*, July 2005.

Dan Brock

"Shaping Future Children: Parental Rights and Societal Interests" *Journal of Political Philosophy*, 2005.

Christopher
Clausen

"Childfree in Toyland," *American Scholar*, Winter 2002.

John Elvin

"Culture Watch: TV Porn And Planned Parenthood," *Insight on the News*, March 19, 2001.

Giulianna
Fuscaldo

"Genetic Ties: Are They Morally Binding?" *Bioethics*, 2006.

Elisabeth Harman

"Can We Harm and Benefit in Creating?" *Philosophical Perspectives*, 2004.

David Heyd

"Male or Female, We Will Create Them: The Ethics of Sex Selection for Non-Medical Reasons," *Ethical Perspectives*, 2003.

Darcus Howe

"The Heroic Struggle of Black Parenthood," *New Statesman*, March 12, 2007.

Jacqueline Kasun

"Population Control Today—And Tomorrow? Saint Margaret Sanger," *World and I*, June 2001.

Avery Kolers   "Cloning and Genetic Parenthood,"
                      *Cambridge Quarterly of Healthcare
                      Ethics*, 2003.

Robert Kuttner   "Body Politics," *The American
                      Prospect*, September 24, 2001.

P. Montague   "The Myth of Parental Rights," *Social
                      Theory and Practice*, 2000.

Cristina Odone   "Parenthood Is No Longer a Matter
                      of Blood; It Has to Be Defined by
                      State Regulation", *New Statesman*,
                      November 11, 2002.

Paul Craig   "Government Intrusion, Sex Culture,
Roberts   Abuse Kids," *Insight on the News*
                      March 5, 2001.

Julian Savulescu   "Procreative Beneficence: Why We
                      Should Select the Best Children,"
                      Bioethics, 2001.

Stephen Scales   "Intergenerational Justice and Care in
                      Parenting," *Social Theory and
                      Practice*, 2002.

Liezl Van Zyl   "Intentional Parenthood and the
                      Nuclear Family," *Journal of Medical
                      Humanities*, 2002.

Simo Vehmas   "Is It Wrong to Deliberately Conceive
                      or Give Birth to a Child with Mental
                      Retardation?" *Journal of Medicine and
                      Philosophy*, 2002.

Washington Times   "Abortions and Planned Parenthood,"
                      Washington Times, April 8, 2008.

Barbara Dafoe Whitehead — "Parenthood: Once the Norm, Now the Exception?" *Commonweal*, June 16, 2006.

Wendy Wright — "Federal Government Should Not Be in the Business of Funding Abortion," *Insight on the News*, October 29, 2001.

Michela Wrong — "Parenthood by Piggyback," *New Statesman*, October 23, 2006.

Index